Teambuilding That Gets Results

ESSENTIAL PLANS AND

ACTIVITIES FOR CREATING

EFFECTIVE TEAMS

LINDA EVE DIAMOND AND HARRIET DIAMOND

SOURCEBOOKS, INC.
NAPERVILLE, ILLINOIS

Published by Sourcebooks, Inc.
P.O. Box 4410, Naperville, Illinois 60567-4410
(630) 961-3900
FAX: (630) 961-2168
www.sourcebooks.com

Library of Congress Cataloging-in-Publication Data
  Library of Congress Cataloging-in-Publication Data

  Diamond, Linda Eve.
  Teambuilding that gets results : essential plans and activities
  for creating effective teams / Linda Eve Diamond and Harriet Diamond.
       p. cm.
   Includes index.
   ISBN-13: 978-1-4022-0746-4
   ISBN-10: 1-4022-0746-8
   1. Teams in the workplace. 2. Interpersonal communication. 3.
  Organizational effectiveness. 4. Business networks. I. Diamond,
  Harriet. II. Title.

  HD66.D53 2007
  658.4'022--dc22

  2006032032

Printed and bound in the United States of America.
BG 10 9 8 7 6 5 4 3 2

Contents

Acknowledgments

We thank each contributor for being part of our team. In true team spirit, these diverse and inspiring role models added depth and dimension to this book that we would not have achieved on our own.

Our many thanks to you: Steven Adubato, James Desena, Tom Terez, Susan Brenner, Mel Silberman, James Neill, Sandra Richardson, Betty Jagoda Murphy, Dino Signore, William Miller, Patricia May, Patty Briguglio, Anne Saunier, Roger Hillman, Matthew Odette, Vadim Kotelnikov, Natalie Gast, Val Boyko, Sondra Sen, Ronald Bell, Lisa Savage, Rochelle Devereaux, Steve Lefkowitz, Kathleene Derrig-Palumbo, Jeffrey D. Zbar, Valerie Shondel, Teresa Weed Newman, John Dennis, Georgann Occipinti, Peter Tomolonis, and Lurita Doane. Our thanks, too, to Monica Smiley, Raylie Dunkel, and Marcia Firestone, who helped build our team by referring us to many rich sources, and to Daniel Libeskind, whose remarks during a lecture inspired our opening chapter.

We could not have completed this project without our own team: Grace Freedson, our agent, for introducing us to Sourcebooks, and to Peter Lynch and Erin Nevius for the free reign to develop our concept for this book and their incisive comments that enhanced it. Last, but never least, our in-house counsel and sounding board, Michael Diamond.

Additional thoughts and thanks from Harriet: Team influence is a cumulative journey. I've been a team leader and a team player in many settings. My thanks to those who mentored me and those who trusted my guidance, to the business organizations that helped me grow and allowed me to lead, to the clients who put their teams in my hands and the training/consulting team that made it possible for me to honor that trust. My most trusted teammate, and surely most patient, is my coauthor and daughter, Linda, whose energy and creativity are reflected in all my work of recent decades.

Additional thoughts and thanks from Linda: First as a team member in her corporate training company, then as her writing partner, I learned, from example, about motivational leadership and teamwork the same place I learned all of life's most valuable lessons—from my mom. Thanks, partner!

Introduction

Building and leading a team that gets results begins with establishing a team mindset, for yourself and your team. For that reason, *Teambuilding That Gets Results* begins with a discussion of what a team is and the essential nature of the team mindset. From there, we lead you through the stages of team development, then team processes and the foundational skills that make teams work, including communication, feedback, and change. We then expand on the culture mix and the virtual team because these elements have become increasingly common, and each presents unique team challenges.

Later chapters offer guidelines for periodically taking stock of your team and expanding your internal team: What are your goals? Is it time to hire? How do you find a good "fit"?

We conclude by asking you to step back to take a broader look at your extended team. Who is or could be on your team? Do you consider only employees "part of your team"? Think beyond the scope of your office (real or virtual); think beyond those on your payroll. Who else has or could have an interest in your business or contribute to your team? You most likely have the makings of a more powerful, results-oriented team than you realize.

Throughout the book, you will find team activities ranging from those designed expressly for teambuilding—forging relationships, building trust, working together from new angles, bonding—to those designed with specific outcomes for business growth. In addition, leadership activities offer guidance and help you keep and refine your perspective as you continue throughout the process of building and strengthening your team. Appendix B provides a list of all activities by chapter for easy reference.

Chapter

1

Teams

"No one can whistle a symphony. It takes an orchestra to play it." —H.E. Luccock

What Is Teamwork?

Teamwork is all around us, in everything we see that is the combined effort or effect of individual forces. Noted architect Daniel Libeskind emphasizes this point about teamwork, relating it to architecture, among other things. He opens his book, *Breaking Ground*, with the following illustration of teamwork: "Someone once asked Goethe what color he liked best. 'I like rainbows,' he said. That's what I love about architecture: If it's good, it's about every color in the spectrum of life; if it's bad, the colors fade away entirely." The expansion of the team notion to rainbows and architecture may seem like an unconventional place to begin a team-building book. Stepping out of convention and out of the traditional ways of seeing, however, often leads us to growth and positive change, so we open here by expanding on those ideas and painting, with broad strokes, an image of team.

Teams at Play

A team is comprised of parts, each forming a support system and working towards a common goal. Often, when we think of teams, we immediately jump to sports analogies—a logical move, but let's look first at more untraditional notions of teams, those working relationships that are so smooth they typically go unnoticed.

Music

A single note played on a sole instrument will not sustain your interest for long; music is nothing without a variety of notes, each with a sound and a precise role in any given piece of music. Together, notes create chords and variations. Every instrument has its own life and breadth of musical capabilities. Most people have a favorite instrument and love to hear a solo on it. Put instruments together in concert, however, and the combined sound is a completely different experience. It's the combination of notes and the musicians themselves and, depending on the piece, a blending of instruments and vocals that create a musical work teeming with emotion.

Architecture

Architecture relies on people to flesh out every aspect and make a building come alive: people concerned with aesthetics, functionality, and city planning; people to crunch the numbers; people to put teams together within the team, people to break ground, pour concrete, and build the final product, which has grown from a thought to three dimensions. As Libeskind reminds us, even the elements of the building itself—every nail, beam, and window—are working together as a team to create the final design. How do the walls, the ceiling, and the floors combine to create support and effect? Nuances of lighting and design add to the total impact. Take a closer look at some of the buildings you are familiar with and take notice of some of the more interesting buildings around you; look at how the parts combine to create the whole.

Cities

In *The Flight of the Creative Class*, Richard Florida talks about cities that attract and exude creativity. His two criteria for this status are: 1) aesthetic character 2) openness, inclusiveness, and tolerance. These are cities that welcome diversity and benefit from it, encourage creativity and bask in its gifts, and bring the energy of these elements to every sector. Cities like these are teamwork in action.

Nature

We have only to look to nature to see the results of teamwork; everything in nature is interconnected. A leaf falling gently to the ground becomes the basis for the next year's soil. Earthworms know to knead the soil and enrich it. Moisture and sunlight bring life to seeds. Harvesting time brings to a crescendo the work of every team member that makes life itself possible.

These unconventional team examples help us realize the importance of all working relationships.

Sports and Teams

Of course, let's not forget sports. Teamwork is the foundation of most sports. In a recent talk, Art Shamsky, former outfielder and first baseman for the New York Mets and author of *The Magnificent Seasons*, recalled how the Mets had one bad season after another until 1969. Then suddenly, they morphed into a team and took off, winning the World Series. In reply to the question of how the Mets achieved their miraculous turnaround, Shamsky simply said that Gil Hodges became the coach, and he pulled the team together. All of those talented ball players could not have won the series unless they coalesced into a team. Contributing to the Mets' success as a team, Shamsky recalls, is that in a time of racial tensions throughout the country, the Mets did not have racial or religious problems among the team members. Still and always, equality and respect are cornerstones of championship-level teams, in any sport and any industry.

Great coaches inspire and help people to be team players; some people have a natural inclination for team play. One example of an outstanding team player was Bob Cousy, a guard for the Boston Celtics. Although he was a great shooter who could easily have taken control of the ball and scored even more than his impressive record, he was known for passing the ball to give others a "shot," literally and figuratively. He revolutionized the game of basketball with his "no-look passes" and "behind-the-back feeds." Former Celtic star Tommy Heinsohn recalls: "Once that ball reached his hands, the rest of us just took off, never bothering to look back. We didn't have to. He'd find us. When you'd go into a position to score, the ball would be there."

Have you ever watched the Olympics' individual sports competitors? Each of those young athletes is supported by coaches, family, and others. No champion goes it alone. Each has a support system: trainers, family, friends, and strangers, even entire countries, cheering them on.

QUICK Tip

Team wisdom: "I love to hear a choir. I love the humanity...to see the faces of real people devoting themselves to a piece of music. I like the teamwork. It makes me feel optimistic about the human race when I see them cooperating like that." —Paul McCartney

What Team?

Most small business owners see themselves as "the business." This is detrimental to the "buy-in" and motivation of those they employ, as well as to the image of the company—both for growth and for the overall value of the business. *Teambuilding That Gets Results* requires not only expanding your sights, your horizons, perhaps your products and services, but also your team. If you're wondering, "What team?" think again.

Business owners with a "What team?" mentality, trying to hold down expenses by doing it all, often miss opportunities. The saying, "You have to spend money to make money" rings true as you grow your business. Investing in human capital pays off. Recognize when the cost of *not* having a solid team is greater than the cost of hiring.

As your business grows, you will probably find that wearing every hat becomes a bit unwieldy. Yes, you know the product or service inside out, so you are the best one to market. You've been involved in design and development since day one, so you must be in charge of that. Who better than the business owner to send out invoices, follow up on late payments, maintain inventory, hire necessary vendors? *Or* how about using some of that time and energy to build a talented team?

Identify key roles and responsibilities and recognize that if you are performing all of them, none is getting done as well as it could. Know your strengths and focus on those. Then, slowly build your human resources. Support staff is crucial to most business growth. Support means "to hold up or add strength to." You can start with part-time help. Consider hiring contract employees. (Be sure to learn about labor laws and legal ramifications.) Use other available resources for brainstorming and problem solving: colleagues, friends, and family. Have you thought about creating an advisory board? (More on hiring and growing your team in chapters 10 and 11.)

The right attitude: Even if you have only two people working with or for you, and only part time, your perspective is important to the creation of a teamwork attitude. You want everyone involved informed about the scope of the work, the clients, your vision, and your goals. Should either employee need assistance with a task or a project, you and the other employee *are* that person's team.

Often, a business grows unplanned, with everyone working to meet increasing demand, unmindful of the expanded workload and growing diversion of priorities that will eventually result in conflict. Creating a team mindset helps prevent, or at least mitigate, potential problems.

Spend money to make money: In the early eighties, we worked with a large supermarket chain that had begun as a mom-and-pop store. Despite the decades of growth, the corporate offices, and the large staff with multiple management layers, the company president continued to run the business as though it were still the corner grocery store, much to the frustration of those working to help the business grow and succeed. His too-tight reign on spending led to poor training and missed opportunities; his insistence on being in every loop tangled those loops and bogged down progress. Meanwhile, the competition moved ahead. Fortunately, time and internal talent ultimately turned the company around.

Teams That Work

Is teambuilding as simple as appreciating a rainbow or quoting sports coaches? Of course not! Teambuilding takes work and an understanding of both group and individual dynamics. We all see examples of teams that don't work: the sports team loses its edge, the band misses notes, communication breaks down in a small office. What's the solution? Should we only listen to one instrument at a time and only watch or play individual (rather than team) sports? Should we take the whole burden of work on our own shoulders because, as they say, "If you want a job done right, do it yourself"? Abandon that notion for this one: If you hire and train talented people, you will free yourself to accomplish more.

While the team dynamic is complex and one individual can have a powerful effect on bringing the team down, the efforts of a working team can be extraordinary, certainly beyond the results achievable by one person. Remember the rainbow effect: each color brings strength to the whole. The same is true of a strong team, with each member performing his or her best for the team.

What is a "sense of team?" It is a feeling of belonging, an understanding that you are all "there" for one another, wherever "there" is. A good team is, in essence, a family—an ideal family. Each cares about the others' well-being, and all work in concert to ensure the best common result. Friction, factions, debates, and agreements occur but don't dominate. The goal: achieving the team's vision.

Another aspect of teams that work is the trust factor, particularly trusting the team leader, especially the company's owner. The basic trust test is: Do you do what you say you will? Can you be believed? Can people rely upon you?

Make your team feel good about coming in to work; it starts with you. The fundamental first step in creating and energizing teams is providing a positive environment. For starters, it is clean, safe, and respectful. That's just basic. Do you make it clear that harassment of any kind will not be tolerated? Do you have safe, simple channels for those who feel they are being treated disrespectfully?

Your level of openness, tone of voice, and overall communication style all contribute to creating a work environment that breeds either harmony or dissonance. Do you use positive language? Encourage the team with positive feedback? Do you build in team members' support of each other as a significant dimension in performance appraisals and evaluations?

Whether your focus right now is on bringing people together for time-framed projects or building and refining the workforce that will conduct your daily business and bring your dream closer to fruition, your goal is to create cohesive teams comprised of skilled, knowledgeable people. Teams that work start with people who feel appreciated, encouraged, and respected. They have leaders who know how to create a positive environment in which each member has the freedom and motivation to contribute to his or her fullest abilities.

QUICK Tip

The trust factor: John Dennis, chairman of HED International, learned about the true nature of teamwork early in his career, working as an engineer with a mining company. He talks about miners as being "the real 'salt of the earth,' working and living closely together in small remote places with names like 'Deep Step.'" Their sense of team is passionate because without one another's support, without an unquestionable ability to trust all team members, no one could descend into that mine each day. Each day, they risk their lives; families know any morning's "good-bye" could be the last. Thus, a strong bond, even a sense of family, develops among the community, the extended team. The same need for unfailing trust exists among firefighters and police officers, others who risk their lives in the line of duty.

How does that trust get translated to the team in an office building, a factory, or retail outlet? How do the stakes matter to that extent? They can't. Nothing cuts to the core of trust more than having your life depend on someone else. But the trust factor can be developed, and we have a lot to learn from people who put their safety in each other's hands. A common teambuilding activity that has been around for decades is having participants pair off and take turns falling backwards, trusting their partners to catch them. Once you can rely on someone for your physical safety, trust deepens; you feel this is someone who won't let you down, won't let you fall—literally *or* figuratively.

Empowering Leadership

You are an entrepreneur. You exhibit the characteristics that drive entrepreneurs toward success: passion, vision, a tolerance for risk, self-confidence, an eye on the big picture, a clear sense of ownership. Imagine a team that has all of these winning factors. That's a team that you can create by instilling a sense of intrapreneurship (the entrepreneurial spirit in the "company" person) in everyone in your organization. Even the largest companies are realizing that employees who have a sense of ownership are more motivated than those who feel that they are only doing someone else's bidding.

As a leader, you want to develop your team to be a strong entity on its own. This means *empowering*: training, teambuilding, trusting, and letting go. Yes, you are the final authority on how your business is run, but looming over shoulders day in and day out, insisting on being the one and only "face of your business" drains both your energy and your team's motivation. Teams and individual team members thrive when they have a sense of ownership. The more empowered people are, the more engaged and the more committed they are to their employers and their work.

Rarely can you hire someone on day one or put someone on a new kind of project and say, "Go get 'em" and walk away. Even the right person, in the right job, with the requisite skills needs some level of orientation and an introduction to your vision, goals, and work culture. Usually, it takes time, more than any entrepreneur wants to spend, to provide the training and supervision to ensure that those on the team have the knowledge, tools, and resources to "take off," but that time is a wise investment. Whether through one-to-one coaching, on-the-job training, mentoring, shadowing (a new team member "shadows" a more experienced one to observe and learn), or seminars (in-house or off-site), employees appreciate your efforts to help them grow and learn.

Empowerment, simply put, gives teams and team members the power they need to perform their jobs successfully. Empowerment goes beyond giving responsibility; it means giving authority, as well. Authority puts the "teeth" in responsibility. It's the difference between an employee wanting to take action and actually taking it. A confident leader is not afraid to give others the space in which to make decisions. With empowerment come the inevitable mistakes; accept that they are often part of the learning curve. An environment that leaves room for mistakes also leaves room for innovation and new solutions.

Within your business, what authority can you empower others with that would make the proverbial wheels turn faster, would create a more efficient flow, and would ultimately increase customer satisfaction? How often have you, as a customer, heard the phrase, "It's not my job," or the perennial favorite, "I don't have the authority to do that."? How often have you seen teams stopped in their tracks waiting for someone with the proper authority to sign off, when it was clear that someone else could easily have been *empowered* to do so? Clearly, there are times when one in a greater position of responsibility and accountability should make the call. However, when the calls could be trusted to a "front line" person, that shift would both streamline processes and strengthen that team member's commitment.

Delegation is a form of empowerment. Whether you are delegating to a team within your organization or an individual who is a part of your team, delegation is not dumping; it is a deliberate, planned passing on of duties and, ultimately, ownership. Determine what responsibilities or tasks would be best carried out by someone else for good reason. Be cognizant that you are building a team. Delegation should not be the runoff of your overload, but part of a building plan for your team, placing team members in key positions in which they are depended on, empowered, and better able to contribute to the team.

Delegate to those you trust: "You can say to those you lead, 'I trust you and I value your opinions.' But this means nothing unless you live it. Rhetoric is easy. Reality is hard. You have to give people the room and the right to make mistakes and learn from them. It's the only way people grow. My television production company is made up of a group of professionals who run that company on a day-to-day basis without me. I have communicated a vision and I am available to every team member at virtually any time, but most often I am out of the office securing sponsorship and creating program ideas. A few years back I changed the way I managed our team—it was the best executive decision I ever made.

I had realized that before sending out memos and letters, my staff was sending every one to me for my approval. They were also holding up critical decisions while waiting for my approval. Each of these people had already demonstrated a level of expertise, professionalism, and intelligence, so I said to them, 'If you are convinced that we need to do something, send me an email or voice mail and tell me why. If I don't get back to you within twenty-four hours, go ahead and do it.' This has been a very liberating arrangement for all of us. They no longer have their hands tied when they need to make decisions and have more information than I do. I no longer have to take the time to give feedback about every single thing that goes on."

—From *Speak from the Heart: Be Yourself and Get Results* by Steven Adubato, PhD with Theresa Foy DiGeronimo, the Free Press/Simon and Schuster ©2002 Steve Adubato

Leadership Activity: Letting Go

Think about all of the hats you wear and the responsibilities you carry out. Write down one that you will gladly delegate to someone else. Think through the process and review the Delegation Checkpoints below. Make your own list of specific steps to take to ensure that the delegation is successful. What information must you share? What skills must you validate? What training must you provide? Now, think of something that you enjoy doing but know that someone else should do it because 1) it is no longer one of your top priorities, 2) another person could do it better, or 3) another will develop the necessary skills through doing it.

Delegation Checkpoints

Have you...

- Delegated the right job to the right person?
- Supervised to see that the job was properly done?
- Observed interactions?
- Given strong, clear feedback and followed up?
- Made your level of availability clear at each stage?
- Clearly established situations where you would like to be consulted?
- Backed away to allow this person to become respected and empowered in the role?

Figure 1.1: 10 LEADERSHIP ESSENTIALS

1. **Create a positive work environment.** You set, maintain, and change the tone. Model and encourage a positive one.

2. **Set clear expectations.** Tell people what you expect, when, and how, or your day can be filled with surprises, such as, "Oh, you meant today?" Unclear expectations create an atmosphere of unease and frustration.

3. **Give clear guidelines.** As others participate in your organization, give them clear road maps. Don't keep your processes a secret.

4. **Delegate.** The added perspective on a job can create even more substantial results than you might create if it were part of your balancing act.

5. **Be enthusiastic.** Enthusiasm is contagious and creates an energetic work environment.

6. **Demonstrate confidence.** Believe in your product/service and yourself. Others will be far more eager to follow you.

7. **Provide necessary resources.** Ensure that team members can access information and people to help them achieve their goals.

8. **Provide training.** Provide team members with the skills and information to reach their fullest potential. If you want your team to be confident and competent, provide avenues for them to enhance their knowledge and skills.

9. **Inspire a team spirit.** Hone your understanding of teams to create a positive atmosphere in which people feel appreciated and inspired.

10. **Provide developmental feedback.** By letting your team know how they are doing, you will propel them to excellence.

Alert!

Setting the tone: A senior vice president at a Fortune 500 company once commented that he typically walked through the building with his mind on the "problem du jour," consequently looking grave and not making eye contact with or smiling at others. He learned through the grapevine that the common perception was that he was always angry. He now keeps his expression in the present, and the general mood in the company is lighter.

Stating Your Vision

Before you can bring others into the fold and empower them to help you realize your vision, you need to be clear about what that vision is and have it stated it in a way that easily helps your team members see where you're heading. Your vision statement is your vision of your company's future. For example, Westin's vision statement: "Year after year, Westin and its people will be regarded as the best and most sought-after hotel and resort management group in North America." The 3M vision: "Achieving Breakthrough Performance for our Customers, Employees, and Shareholders." Can Westin really expect to be, unequivocally, the most universally sought-after in North America? Can 3M guarantee that it will continue to achieve breakthrough performance year after year? These might sound idealized, but your vision is the ideal for which you and your team strive, so set the bar high.

What about mission? A brief mission statement that can easily energize, motivate, and actually be remembered is best. 3M's mission: "To solve unsolved problems innovatively." The mission statement is typically followed by values to ensure that the mission is carried out without compromising the company's core values. The following examples illustrate two ways this can be done. Mary Kay's statement, below, is followed by a short paragraph, while Disney uses bullet points. Use your own style. Form is far less important than substance.

Examples:

Mary Kay Cosmetics

"To give unlimited opportunity to women."

We will do this in tangible ways, by offering quality products to consumers, financial opportunities to our independent sales force, and fulfilling careers to our employees. We will also reach out to the heart and spirit of women, enabling personal growth and fulfillment for the women whose lives we touch. We will carry out our mission in a spirit of caring, living the positive values on which our company was built."

Walt Disney
- "To make people happy."

Disney's Values:
- No cynicism
- Nurturing and promulgation of "wholesome American values"
- Creativity, dreams, and imagination
- Fanatical attention to consistency and detail
- Preservation and control of the Disney "magic"

QUICK Tip

Promote your mission: Often, business owners or others in leadership positions assume they have a clear mission and that their team is committed to it. Having clarity and commitment to what you want to accomplish is too critical to take for granted. You may believe that you do. But, do others understand it as you do? Many business owners believe that they have shared their mission and vision with those who work with them and are surprised to learn that others "just don't get it."

I was consulting for a bank president on team issues when he asked his assembled team, "How many of you understand what our mission is?" Not one hand shot into the air. He next asked, "How many know that we have a mission statement?" The same lack of response followed. He then left the room and came back with a beautiful wooden plaque with a brass plate on which the bank's mission statement was engraved and held it up for the group to see. It was long, about three-quarters of a page too long.

—James Desena, Merritt Island Florida-based consultant and author of *The 10 Immutable Laws of Power Selling*, www.salesleaders.com

Figure 1.2: **BUZZWORD BONANZAS**

Q: What exactly is the difference between a mission statement and a vision statement, and how can ours be world-class?

A: There is a critically important difference between these two key ingredients of an effective organization. A recent study, conducted by the American Association of People Who Don't Mind and In Fact Advocate Long-Windedness in Their Communications, showed that the typical mission statement includes two semicolons, two dashes, and at least two business buzzwords—while the vision statement contains only one dash but makes up for it with at least one run-on sentence. To be at all credible, a company's mission and vision statements combined must include at least five of the following terms and phrases:

high-performance

world-class

diversity

empowerment

employees are our most important asset

exceeds

delight(s)

right the first time

everyone's job

puts people first

puts the customer first

puts employee bonuses first

—Tom Terez, speaker, workshop leader, and author of the book *22 Keys to Creating a Meaningful Workplace*, betterworkplacenow.com and TomTerez.com

Find the right motivation: When Susan Brenner EdD, senior vice president of Bright Horizons Family Solutions (providers of early care and education solutions) joined the company, it had only three on-site programs in corporations. She now oversees several divisions of the six hundred-plus corporate child-care centers and schools run by this multimillion-dollar organization.

Bright Horizons' leadership, knowing the value of a teamwork company culture, created the HEART principles through a management team effort to guide and support all members in their work. Once each principle had been carefully articulated, the team developed heart cards and case studies that reflected the principles, and it rolled out the concept at an off-site retreat for eight hundred directors. Groups competed to resolve the case-study issues.

"The energy and sense of mutual purpose created by that event, with two teams competing at each table, was the foundation for our strong, company-wide commitment to these principles," stated Susan. The eight hundred attendees went on to train others throughout the organization to instill these lasting, guiding principles, ensuring that all team members reflected the company's spirit. With this initiative, Bright Horizons reinforced the work environment created to support its mission: *to provide innovative programs that help children, families, and employers work together to be their very best.*

Teeming with Teams

As a business owner, your primary team is your team-of-the-whole, your organization. Within your organization may be departments, committees, and project teams. These teams within the team are essential to the success of your team-of-the-whole. No matter what size your company, creating smaller teams within it helps ensure that someone always has an eye on the several focus areas of your business and that you have a trusted collaborator or two, someone with whom to generate ideas and solve problems.

Depending on the company's size and culture, teams vary. Take, for example, a hotel. First, every employee is a member of the team and within that team are departments: operations, marketing, food services, housekeeping, maintenance, engineering, finance, human resources, and security. Within each of those departments are teams that come together based on shifts or management requests for special projects.

No part operates in isolation from the whole. Ideally, each team within the team (and teams within those teams) functions to meet departmental goals that fit in with the company's overall vision. As you can imagine, these multiple teams will be your downfall if you do not create clear communication channels within and among them. Depending on the organization's size, cross-functional teams can ensure that each department understands, assists, and works in concert with others.

Even without departments, you have (or soon will have) individuals with specific strengths and responsibilities. Create multiple teams among the smallest number of employees. Through regular staff meetings, each person reports on his/her progress and problems and can call upon others for assistance, creating ad hoc teams as necessary.

Now switch from the microscope to the telescope. Your team as a whole is part of your community, your industry sector, and the world; even local companies gain international exposure through the World Wide Web. You also have teams that extend beyond your team and teams that intersect with yours. Do you have an accountant or web designer who works with someone on your team? That working group is another team. What about others who have an interest in your business? Vendors and contractors? Do you ever collaborate with other businesses or organizations?

Your business is not independent of all outside factors and influences. No business is an island. Your team is teeming with teams that are part of the larger construct, and your team itself is part of a larger construct, as well. As you grow, you may establish partnerships and alliances to reach broader markets. The opportunities for teams-within-teams are enormous.

Teams must be symbiotic: The hotel manager, Sarina, was facing a challenge. She had an aggressive sales and marketing manager who was bringing in groups for conferences beyond anyone's wildest dreams. Jose was personable and dedicated. Clients loved him, especially for his willingness to "throw in extras." His sales team got the message and contracts poured in; however, each contract had a special twist, a unique substitution, or an unexpected extra. The sales and marketing team was ecstatic. Each time they finished one round of contracts, they were on to the next.

Who wouldn't be thrilled? The food and beverage department manager, Sal. His department had a system for events. They worked well as a team and each knew what to do, when, and how. Suddenly, everything was in chaos. Sal was beside himself. "Since when do we serve soup *or* salad with a conference lunch? Do you know how getting those choices will throw us off? All of a sudden, we're a five-star restaurant catering to the hoity-toity. This is a conference, with a *menu* and a *schedule!*"

Sarina had to do something. She didn't want to lose the business. She didn't want an internal revolution, either. She pulled together a team meeting with all of her department heads. They focused on internal customer service: How can each department best serve the others? What do they need to know about how the others' function? What deadlines for sharing information would facilitate smooth team interactions?

During this exchange, Jose learned that his promises to these conference groups affected many departments negatively, despite the increase in sales. Sarina scheduled a second meeting specifically to apply the information and decisions of the larger meeting to clusters of departments that needed to work through solutions. With clear expectations of one another and realistic deadlines, Jose and Sal reached a number of compromises that continue to improve the quality of their service and create a more peaceful working environment.

Leadership Activity: Assess Your Team

Periodic assessments are helpful tools, for both you and your team members. What is your assessment of your current team? Use the following assessment now as a starting place for building your team for results; think of it as a baseline, which can be used again to monitor progress and to serve as a reminder to keep critical team issues on track.

Answer each of the following with a score of 1, 2, or 3.

1 = True   2 = Sometimes True   3 = Not True for Our Team

Organization

The team knows exactly what has to get done.

Each member of the team has a clear idea of the team goals.

Team members are clear about their roles within the team.

The team holds regular, effective meetings.

Supportive Atmosphere

Team members who offer new ideas get a lot of support and encouragement.

Team members freely express their real views.

All team members demonstrate respect for each other.

Everyone's opinion gets listened to.

There is healthy debate among team members but very little bickering.

Methods for Troubleshooting and Change

The team has clear channels for concerns or complaints.

The team has a working method for resolving conflict.

If a team member leaves or is suddenly out sick, other team members know how to access key information and can pick up critical pieces.

Team members are open to new ideas.

Team members don't arbitrarily discard what is working for something else just because it's new.

Team Spirit

Team members are excited about the project/mission/goals.

Team members know that they each play a valuable part in the project/mission/goals.

Team members understand that challenges are opportunities to make improvements, be creative, and use their talents and abilities to the fullest.

What's the Score?

1–25 Congratulations! Your team is already soaring and scoring high.

26–35 Your team has many of the basic foundations in place but needs some work to refine.

36–45 Your team needs major reorganization and reaffirmation of roles and goals. Let them know you are ready to make changes.

46–51 You don't need a book to tell you your team isn't working, but it's not too late to realign the team. You'll have a lot to do to motivate this team, but let them know you're in it with them, committed to making changes. Start by taking suggestions and feedback from the team.

For any score, note those areas in which you had the most 3s, then the most 2s. Go through the entire book using team and leadership activities, but focus particular attention on those trouble spots.

Use those trouble spots to fill in the following team profile, and also what you know about your team that may not have been in the assessment. Only you know your team's strengths and challenges. Before you continue, take a moment to think about how you might capitalize on strengths and overcome challenges. Come back to this profile as you continue through the book and through building your team.

Team Profile

Team Strengths:

_____

_____

_____

_____

What can I do to build and capitalize on these strengths?

_____

_____

_____

Team Challenges:

_____

_____

_____

What can I do to help my team and individual team members overcome these challenges?

_____

_____

_____

Chapter

Team Development

"Michael, if you can't pass, you can't play." —Coach Dean Smith to Michael Jordan in his freshman year at UNC

▶ Take Charge of Your Team

▶ Stages of Team Development

▶ What Stage Is Your Team in Now?

Take Charge of Your Team

Your business is an evolving team. Teams may exist and function within the whole, but the business itself is a critical team. As a business owner, recognize your role in creating cohesion or, perhaps, inadvertently sabotaging it. Chances are, you started as a team of one or a team that included you and one or two loyal supporters. Your team may have developed with little conscious formation; however, rarely does a group of people start operating as a team without a little planning and guidance. The good news is that it's never too late to form, refine, or energize your team.

Stages of Team Development

While the stages of development below speak specifically, at times, to project teams, the stages also apply to a work team that is ongoing—your staff. Though your staff, as a unit, is an entity with a less defined "beginning" and "end," the phases are still useful. If your team is not working well, start at the beginning, with "forming" to reassess and refine everyone's place on the team.

Most teams progress through logical stages. If you have attended teambuilding seminars or read other books on teambuilding, you might already be acquainted with these well-known stages of development:

- Forming (team is formed, roles are defined)
- Storming (areas of conflict become apparent)
- Norming (team adjusts and finds methods of compromise)
- Performing (team is working at maximum efficiency to produce results)
- Adjourning (disbanding the team)

This model was first introduced in 1965 by Bruce Tuckman and, though often modified, is still the most widely used model in the corporate training industry. We believe this model has endured over time because it produces a simple, precise illustration of how a strong team forms and evolves.

Not all teams progress to the end stages; most ineffective teams have not gotten organized or cohesive enough to move beyond the early ones. Your role is critical during the "forming" stage. Think carefully about how your current team has evolved as you go forward to create a new dynamic. Well-founded teams that function at high levels begin with solid leadership.

Notice the changing leadership role through the stages of team development. The balance of power from a leader to a team is a slow, deliberate shift with checkpoints along the way. The best teams are autonomous and able to make and execute decisions; however, many teams don't start out that way. In the "forming" stage, a supervisor (manager, business owner) is responsible for pulling the team together, answering questions, and setting the broad course before the team begins to develop leadership, skill, and autonomy within itself. The leader's level of involvement in the beginning should be in inverse proportion to the level of involvement once the team is in full operation in the "norming" and "performing" stages.

Figure 2.1: **TEAM LEADERSHIP OPTIONS**

Many factors come into play as you determine leadership modes for project or other naturally formed or ad hoc teams, including interpersonal dynamics, project time frames, virtual/face-to-face factors, and your own delegation style and comfort level. Feel free to experiment as long as you transition carefully; never take leadership away suddenly, publicly, or without careful explanation. All options below are viable and any one may be best suited to a particular team or circumstance.

You: As with your permanent team, you may be the natural one to start the team, the go-to person, and the one to lead the group all the way through the process.

Leadership delegated by you: You can take a step back and empower a team member whom you trust with a leadership position, which leaves you more in the role of a team leader consultant.

Leadership chosen by the team: If you have a solid, capable team that has worked on similar projects, one option is to develop guidelines for establishing leadership within the team. This is tricky and you may need to monitor the process to ensure that egos do not make it counterproductive. However, the more a team "invents" itself, the more team members feel a sense of ownership and buy in.

A system of rotating leadership: In a system of rotating leadership for key teams, your leadership role (though more background than forefront) may be ongoing and apparent as the team is in continual state of flux. Rotating leadership is the most difficult, but can also be highly rewarding. The pitfalls are discontinuity—a continual state of leaders finding balance and changing rules. The benefits are fresh perspectives and a lack of complacency. For this system to work, however, smooth transitioning and a few unshakable ground rules are essential to keep the team focused and minimize the downsides.

QUICK Tip

Team wisdom: "Wearing the same shirts doesn't make you a team." —Buchholz and Roth, authors of *Creating the High Performance Team*

Stage 1: Forming

Once operating smoothly, every group has its own customs and unspoken rules. For team members to create that dynamic and work together productively, they need to initially establish ground rules. During the first phase of team development, team members are getting to know each other and defining their roles within the group. Early bonding, settling issues, and creating guidelines lays the groundwork for building a sturdy team.

Necessary Actions

Establish ground rules. This may seem simplistic; however, agreeing to specific guidelines for brainstorming ideas, engaging in debate, disagreeing, reaching consensus, meeting deadlines, and knowing when to move on will simplify the team effort.

Clarify mission and purpose. Does the team have a reason to exist? If that is not clear and accepted by all, team members will have a nagging sense of "Why are we here?" Everyone is busy, and another team and another series of meetings must be purposeful and efficient.

Set goals. In addition to the team's vision and purpose, individuals also need to know what useful personal contribution they can make. They need to fit the team purpose into their value system and their daily tasks. Establishing goals allows people to see the concrete results for which the team is striving. Include in this discussion a plan for celebrating the achievement of team goals.

Assess resources. What knowledge, skills, and abilities (KSAs) does each team member bring to the table? Should others be involved, either directly or indirectly? Know what internal and external resources are available to help your team reach its goals: money, equipment, others' knowledge, skills, and abilities.

Formulate individual roles within the group. Key to the forming stage is determining each team member's role toward achieving the team's purpose. Roles should reflect the KSAs.

Emotional Vibe

The atmosphere can be one of excitement, enthusiasm, concern, anxiety, or a combination of all these emotions. Uncertainty about purpose, roles, decisions, and potential hierarchical situations may cause stress or put people on edge. Team members do not yet have the roles and authority that will build confidence and motivation, so be patient with impatience.

Potential Trouble Spots

Defensiveness. Whether your team is comprised of a small staff, a department, or a company of hundreds or thousands, every team member has a stake in his/her opinions, judgments, and agendas. Many who are used to "the way things were" are not eager to go forward with new formations or new ideas.

Control issues. Within the three-person office and the mega company, "turf" is "turf." A team meeting of three to discuss a change in online or hard copy filing systems can have the same emotional charge as the cross-functional team determining the best use of limited funds.

Initial personality clashes. Preconceptions, past interactions, or just plain distrust of the "new face," can derail a team meeting.

Vision clashes. If everyone's vision of success is different, goal achievement will be virtually impossible.

Alert!

Respect the system in place: Don't be afraid to deconstruct and reform, but be sensitive to those who have already taken ownership of certain responsibilities or projects. A total "wipe the slate clean" approach can demotivate those who have already invested time and energy. Also, because you already have a working team, get input from them on what they believe is working or not working, what talents they would like to express, and what areas they feel qualified to address. Encourage focus on the work product and/or concept, and steer people away from interpersonal issues. Initiate open dialogue to ensure that all perspectives have their moment in the sun during this trying phase of change.

QUICK Tip

Smarter goals: The team is formed to achieve certain goals. Refining the target and goal setting is part of the early team process. In order to meet those goals, each team member must also set individual goals to that end. Business trainers and authors have been teaching for years that goals should be SMART. Recently, this business basics classic has been made SMARTER.

Specific

Measurable

Attainable

Realistic

Time-framed

Elastic

Recorded

Once goals are established, the team should ensure that the final goal statement reflects all SMARTER goal criteria.

Share your team's goals with those outside the immediate team who may be asked to participate at some stage. Remember the "team-of-the-whole" concept from the first chapter's "Teeming with Teams" section (pages 18–19). Your team's goals are not set or achieved in a vacuum. The most effective leaders and teams hold the larger picture in mind.

Team Activity: Why Are We Here?

The following exercise helps clarify your business's or team's mission, vision, or a particular goal to the team members and assures that they understand you or the team leader. It allows people to express their views anonymously and ensures creative input from everyone.

Have each person write on a separate sheet of paper the mission, vision, or goal of your team (or business). Ask that they do not share with one another or write their names on the page.

Collect the papers and redistribute them randomly, giving one to each team member. Then have each team member call out what is written on the sheet he/she received as you or someone else lists the responses on a flip chart. (Some people in the group may try to guess through the handwriting whose sheet they received, but ask the group to respect confidentiality.)

Look at the list with your team. Ask your team what they observe about the list. Be patient in waiting for responses. Are the responses on target? Are most of them the same? If so, you are in good shape. Do you have a variety? Then, you have work to do.

Share your mission, vision, or goal. Discuss why it is important to you and get feedback. Should you revise it to accommodate some of the elements that others suggested? Do you need to shorten it? Does it connect to something that people can believe in and feel good about? People want to be part of a greater good.

—Contributed by James Desena, Merritt Island Florida-based consultant and author of *The 10 Immutable Laws of Power Selling*, www.salesleaders.com

Stage 2: Storming

The second phase, aptly called "storming," is often marked by interpersonal conflict. Team members are making decisions about what the team should do and what individual roles should be. They are asking questions and negotiating tasks. This can be a creative and productive time if team members are comfortable enough to state their ideas and are open to new solutions. This necessary phase, when guided by ground rules and implemented in an open, supportive environment, sets the stage for productive teamwork.

Necessary Actions

Encourage sharing and listening. Gain a greater understanding of one another and the developing team structure. Understanding comes from dialogue.

Establish trust. Trust is established by sticking to your word, following through, and returning calls and emails within a reasonable time frame. ("Reasonable" being a subjective term, the group should clarify what "reasonable" response time frames are.)

Create a culture that appreciates ideas and input. Sensitivity may surround reactions to new ideas; some will gain acceptance and others won't. Listen and ensure that group decisions are based on goals, resources, and facts.

Develop a working support system. Encourage team members to assist each other as they work through their own "pieces of the puzzle." Be available for dialogue and troubleshooting.

Set individual goals. Each team member needs individual goals that support the team goals.

Stay focused on team goals, even through the worst of storming. Remaining focused on team goals keeps even the most heated debates on target and productive.

Reach compromises to move forward. Compromise does not mean, "no one wins." A skillful compromise combines the best of everyone's ideas and forges a new path that no one might have found alone.

Regularly summarize and circulate decisions to ensure understanding. Summarize decisions, actions, and which team members agreed to what task.

Emotional Vibe

Storming can be an emotional time when building a team. Bringing together, for a common purpose, individuals with different motivations, visions, and personality types is bound to create some friction. This is a normal part of the evolution and, in healthy team development, a phase that will settle into the next phase: "norming."

Potential Trouble Spots

Lack of progress. Depending upon the team composition and the goals, progress can be slow. Remember that time spent ironing out problems at this stage is invaluable later.

Formation of cliques and factions. Often, in a larger team, smaller groups or pairs will be more efficient than the entire team moving lockstep every inch of the way. Distinguish between a healthy sub team and a clique. A clique does not share its progress or ideas; cliques thrive on exclusion.

Power struggles. Cross-functional teams may be prone to power struggles. "Will my department get credit or visibility?" often becomes more important than, "What's the best way to reach our goal?" Individuals on a team may bring personal agendas that conflict with one another or the team goals.

Anger and frustration. During the potentially volatile storming stage, tempers may flare and misunderstandings can cause hard feelings and impede progress. Always maintain focus on the task and not on personalities.

Getting stuck. A team can get stuck in this stage if the trouble spots are not addressed and methods of reaching compromise are not established.

Keep on track: Perpetual storming is unproductive. Enforce ground rules. Model and encourage open communication. Discourage and intercept personal attacks.

Periodic team member self-assessments strengthen the team by helping team members recognize problem areas. One way to keep teams on track is to distribute the "Are You a Collaborator?" self-assessment below, which is designed to help individuals evaluate their own skills as team members.

Team Activity: Are You a Collaborator?

Contributed by Mel Silberman, author and president of Active Training, Princeton, NJ, www.activetraining.com.

As a member of a team, unit, or department, there are a number of actions you can take to contribute to the team's overall success. Rate how frequently you engage in the behaviors below.

Do You...

Pitch in and assist others?

1- never

2- seldom

3- occasionally

4- often

Interact with quiet or new teammates?

1- never

2- seldom

3- occasionally

4- often

Encourage teammates who are in conflict to talk out their differences?

1- never

2- seldom

3- occasionally

4- often

Share credit you receive for a job well done?

1- never

2- seldom

3- occasionally

4- often

Suggest teambuilding/problem-solving techniques you may know?

1- never

2- seldom

3- occasionally

4- often

Check to see how your decisions might affect others?

1- never

2- seldom

3- occasionally

4- often

Include everyone in the information loop?

1- never

2- seldom

3- occasionally

4- often

Seek information and expertise of others?

1- never

2- seldom

3- occasionally

4- often

Communicate your own activity so that it is public knowledge?

1- never

2- seldom

3- occasionally

4- often

Inform others of what they can do to support your efforts and ask them to tell you when they need help?

1- never

2- seldom

3- occasionally

4- often

Total _____

Interpreting Your Score

Compare your total score to the ranges below:

30–40: You see yourself as having strong, effective collaborative behaviors and you use them consistently.

20–30: You believe you make some effort to collaborate with others, but see room for improvement.

10–20: You know you're in trouble, but at least you're willing to admit it!

Also, review your rating for each item on the list, with the following thinking points:

1. Pitch in and assist others.

We all have our own job to do, but there may be moments when we can take the time to help others when they need our support. Look for opportunities to lend a hand. Maybe you have a special talent or skill others need. Even if you don't, a helping hand is always appreciated.

2. Interact with quiet or new teammates.

In any group, there are people who are more reticent than others. If group members don't engage such people, it becomes even more difficult for them to open up and become "part of the team." Look for opportunities, both during group meetings or during times when it's more one-on-one, to make these people feel included. Converse with them and seek their opinions.

3. Encourage teammates who are in conflict to talk out their differences.

One of the most valuable things you can do in any work group situation is to help people who are in conflict with each other to resolve their issues directly between themselves. Often what happens is that people keep their distance from any squabbles among group members or allow one of the parties to vent and complain to them as a safe third party. Look for opportunities to encourage direct communication between the combatants.

4. Share credit you receive for a job well done.

When public figures receive awards, they typically thank those who helped them achieve success. Sometimes, such a gesture may come across as just a moment of modesty or social grace, but it doesn't have to be that way. Others usually deserve part of the credit. In work situations, the same requirement occurs. When the credit is shared, the recipients feel appreciated and motivated to support your efforts in the future. Look for opportunities to acknowledge, both publicly and privately, the help and support you obtain from others.

5. Suggest teambuilding and problem-solving techniques you may know.

Have you read, experienced, or received training in teambuilding techniques such as brainstorming, problem analysis, process checking, consensus building, and so forth? Any team tool you know may be very beneficial to a group you work with. It is not necessary to be the team leader to suggest a different process. Any member can. Look for opportunities where the group may benefit from a process you may know.

6. Check to see how your decisions might affect others.

We often don't realize that a decision we make may negatively impact our colleagues. Review some recent decisions you have made, and consider how they might affect others. Put yourself in their shoes. Do any of your decisions create inconvenience for others? Convey lack of interest or support? Lower morale? Cause new problems for others?

7. Include everyone in the information loop.

Among colleagues, no one needs to know everything you know or think. However, there are plenty of situations where information you have would be helpful or even essential to others. Even if, at first glance, the matter only pertains to you, consider whether your colleagues might benefit from this knowledge in the long run. Will it help them do their jobs better? Will the information help them to support your own job performance?

8. Seek information and the expertise of others.

There are two reasons to seek the information and expertise of others: a) others may help you do your job better and b) others bring unique talents to the team. Take stock of the talents of others, especially when they are underutilized, and invite new contributions.

9. Communicate your own activity so that it is public knowledge.

Just as information and your private decisions often need to be shared for the sake of the team, simply letting others know about any actions you have recently undertaken may be important. Maybe you have had an interesting experience that should be shared. Maybe you are involved in a project or assignment that, if shared, would be of interest or benefit to colleagues.

10. Inform others of what they can do to support your efforts and ask them to tell you when they need help.

This is the boldest collaborative action on this list. It is critical that colleagues know what you need from them. Giving this feedback may feel awkward at first, but it gets easier to muster the courage once you've done it. Be sure to return the favor and ask others what you can do for them as well.

Team Activity: Amoeba Race

This fun game, based on the basic biology of a cell, requires cooperation, competition, and close physical interaction. It is a simple activity that helps a group get comfortable with one another and encourages cooperation. The group forms the three parts of an amoeba: protoplasm, cell wall, and nucleus. Then the group travels, splits into two amoebas, and the amoebas have a race.

Step 1: Explain the three parts of an amoeba and allow team members to take their roles in forming one:

• A lot of protoplasm (people who don't mind being close, gather together)

• A cell wall (people who like to contain themselves and others, surround the protoplasm, facing outward, linking arms)

• A nucleus (someone with good eyesight and the ability to keep on top of things should be the nucleus, seated on the shoulders of some of the protoplasm)

Once the amoeba is formed, try taking a walk through a field or around the block. A rhythmic chant might be helpful for coordinating movements. (What sort of sound does a one-celled creature make?)

Finally, try a little cell division. Split into two, create a second nucleus, and have an Amoeba Race.

Protoplasm
Cell wall
Nucleus

—Adapted from "Amoeba Race" by James Neill, researcher, lecturer, adventurer of the mind and planet, www.wilderdom.com

Stage 3: Norming

By this phase, team members have resolved the storms of conflict that marked the previous stage. They have found ways to work together and can concentrate on tasks at hand. The team is beginning to work as a unit, bound by trust, support, and a working routine that will be strengthened as they enter the next stage.

Necessary Actions

Move as a "whole" toward team goals. The goals are now clear; the path toward achieving them is emerging. The team is becoming unified and directed.

Diagnose and solve problems. The trust created allows team members to voice and explore diverse opinions and solutions.

Bring out team and individual strengths. No team can function as a homogeneous entity, moving at a uniform pace through every challenge. Team members will surface at different times with strengths that move the team forward. The best way to foster these strengths is to acknowledge them.

Emotional Vibe

Comfort results from familiarity and teamwork protocols becoming second nature. Team members are comfortably settled into roles and responsibilities. Some aspects of the "storming" phase may surface, but advancement rarely happens in a perfectly straight upward line. As long as the issues are resolved through established channels, the team is progressing. Norming does not mean the end of debate. However, during this phase, efforts should be directed more toward the goal and less toward the team itself. Time devoted in the last phase to smoothing out interpersonal problems or "turf" issues was time well spent.

Potential Trouble Spots

Groupthink. Team members may be so determined to avoid further conflict that they hold back ideas and avoid delicate situations. Efforts to "get along" can result in groupthink, a phenomenon that inhibits fresh, creative ideas.

Complacency. "Business as usual" can stifle progress or inhibit innovation. Having developed a strong team, don't set it loose to just smooth out the rough spots in an existing plan. Be open to innovation.

Accentuate the positive: Congratulate team members on arriving at this stage. Emphasize the importance of continued productive questioning and debate. Review team goals. Are they still on target? Are the goals still SMARTER? Elicit recommendations for adjustments.

Team Activity: How Are We Doing? A Team's Self-Assessment

Suggestions:

1. Distribute the assessment to each member to complete individually. Have all team members score their own assessments.

2. Collect all assessments anonymously and tally responses.

3. Meet with your team to share totals, tallied responses, and comments, and discuss team strengths and weaknesses.

4. Brainstorm strategies for building on strengths and addressing weaknesses. This step is the beginning of your teambuilding process.

5. Follow through, as always, to bring about positive change.

The Assessment

Answer each of the following with a score of 1, 2, or 3.

1 = True

2 = Sometimes True

3 = Not True for Our Team Organization

Organization

The team knows exactly what has to get done.

I have a clear idea of the team goals.

I am clear about my role within the team.

The team holds regular, effective meetings.

Supportive Atmosphere

Team members who offer new ideas get a lot of support and encouragement.

I freely express my real views.

All team members demonstrate respect for each other.

I feel my opinions are listened to.

There is healthy debate among team members but very little bickering.

Methods for Troubleshooting and Change

The team has clear channels for concerns or complaints.

The team has a working method for resolving conflict.

If a team member leaves or is suddenly out sick, other team members know how to access key information and can pick up critical pieces.

Team members are open to new ideas.

Team members don't arbitrarily discard what is working for something just because it's new.

Team Spirit

I am excited about the project/mission/goals.

I feel I play a valuable part in the project/mission/goals.

I understand that challenges are opportunities to make improvements, be creative, and use my talents and abilities to the fullest.

What's the Score?

1–13 Congratulations! Your team is already soaring and scoring high.

14–22 Your team has many of the basic foundations in place, but needs some work to refine.

23–30 Review roles and goals. Your team needs recentering and may need reorganization.

31–39 Your team is struggling, but it's not too late to realign. Work as a team, with your team leader's guidance, to zero in on problems and create solutions. Use your assessment answers as a starting point. What's working and what isn't? What are the problems? It may take time to regroup and strengthen, but being open with your team leader about problems, concerns, and glitches is the first step toward initiating change. Second, consider what you can do to help the situation.

For any score, note those areas in which you had the most 1s, then the most 2s. As you and your team work to strengthen your process, use these scores as a guideline to see what areas you need to work on.

Game Plan

1. When I look at my team's average (not the total), I am satisfied/dissatisfied with the way the team is working together.
2. The item on the assessment that we need to work on most is _____.
3. This item needs attention because _____.
4. The section that needs the most attention is _____.
5. My best idea for strengthening the team is _____.

Stage 4: Performing

In this stage, team members are knowledgeable, comfortably interdependent, motivated, and able to work smoothly together. The team has working mechanisms for decision-making and troubleshooting and has developed clear channels for disagreements and complaints.

Team members have learned to maintain positive relations, get the job done, and deal with conflicts as they arise. They can challenge each other's ideas without getting personal. Operating at peak performance, they are proud of their successes. At this phase, the team appears not to need a leader. However, a need to maintain the enthusiasm and momentum of a peak-performing team by providing new challenges and opportunities for skill development remains.

Necessary Actions

- Continue to move as a "whole" toward team goals.
- Continue to diagnose and solve problems.
- Take full advantage of team and individual strengths.
- Maintain an atmosphere that encourages open dialogue.

Emotional Vibe

The team has reached benchmark success, knows how to function smoothly, and knows it has the dynamic to achieve; it also knows how to handle rough spots. Team members are working together toward the ultimate goal.

Potential Trouble Spots

• **Backsliding.** Even the most effective teams may revert to earlier stages under pressure or in the face of unexpected change. Maintain your support structure so that as the team goes forward, each member still has the support and encouragement of others. Also, the execution of an idea is often different from the conception. The conception usually takes place during an energetic discussion with each team member building on another's ideas; the enthusiasm is palpable. Turning that idea into reality may involve convincing others of its value or benefit.

• **Balance through change.** Leadership may change for any one of several reasons, should a team continue long term. A change in leadership will likely revert the team, temporarily, to storming as team members renegotiate their places and establish a revised team dynamic.

Alert!

Go with the flow: As your staff grows, the dynamic of your workplace changes. You may have spent months or years establishing protocols and systems as well as developing an internal culture and an external image that reflect your goals and values. Don't be surprised or dismayed as new employees question "what was" and "what is." New people coming in change the team dynamic and can temporarily disrupt a team's flow. An understanding of team dynamics will help ease the adjustment and guide the team back to the stage it was in before the disruption.

QUICK Tip

Fast forward: Sometimes a team must come together quickly to solve a short-term or emergency issue. These teams race through the stages as though they are on fast-forward. Ideally, the team would move through the stages, in some form (issues of trust building and bonding can hardly happen in a day), even at accelerated rates. However, a team may not work through its storming issues at lightning speed, so one that has only a few days to work through an issue may find itself working with rather than through the storming stage. The key is to understand that these trouble spots are natural, and the pressures are especially strong in tight time frames. Heighten communication in order to move quickly and be productive.

Stage 5: Adjourning

Even if you are familiar with Tuckman's stages, you may not have heard of this final stage, which he added some years later. This stage is also referred to as "Deforming" and "Mourning." Adjourning, as you know, is the breaking up of the team after the desired outcome is achieved or the set time frame has ended. Teams established for specific purposes adjourn, or move to a less structured model to monitor outcomes. An office staff that develops into a working team does not disband. It may have numerous metamorphoses but will remain intact, with additions or replacements as time passes.

Necessary Actions

Closure. Why was the team formed? Did it accomplish its goal(s)? Who requested the team's actions? To whom does the team report? Is a final report in order? Is an evaluation procedure in place?

Farewell and thank you! The team, formally or informally, should have an opportunity to review a job well-done (or critique a job gone awry) and share appreciation for their efforts.

Emotional Vibe

If the goal was, in fact, achieved, individuals can move on feeling good about their accomplishments and contributions to the team. Be aware of the human aspects of breaking down the team, and be sensitive to potential trouble spots.

Potential Trouble Spots

Bonding has taken place. Breaking up the team may be difficult for some. People who are uncomfortable with change are going through another change—dissolution of the team. People may have come from different locations to work on a project and will not get together again in the near future or, perhaps, ever.

A routine that was created with great effort is now being broken—a likely source of stress, especially for those who are averse to change. Think about maintaining the team for future projects, if that works, or keeping certain members of the team together. As much as possible, the team structure should remain fluid so that everyone has someone to assist when needed.

Ownership issues. Once a team has achieved its goal(s) and put its work in the hands of those who must follow through, some may have trouble letting go. A clearly articulated plan should survive the next step.

QUICK Tip

Time to grieve: Adjourning is an important stage to recognize and respect, even when it's only one member of the team adjourning. The team dynamic is changed, and someone who was part of the ongoing routine is leaving. This shift is important to recognize and gives employees an opportunity to say goodbye as a team and, if appropriate (if the person leaving is promoted or leaving for a positive personal reason), celebrate.

What Stage Is Your Team in Now?

Now that you've reviewed the stages of team development and the necessary actions, potential trouble spots, and emotional vibes, can you identify which stage your team is now in? Maybe all critical points won't match up, but give thought to them to help you recognize your team's current stage.

Leadership Activity: What Stage Is Your Team In?

Actions we are now taking:

-

-

-

Trouble spots (real and potential):

-

-

-

Emotional vibes:

-

-

-

Conclusion:

_____ Forming

_____ Storming

_____ Norming

_____ Performing

_____ Adjourning

If you have not reached the performing stage, review the chapter and think about positive steps to take to get your team there. If you have reached performing, but have a few glitches, take the time to work through them. Don't bump along.

Next steps:

-
-

Chapter

Team Processes

"The best way to have a good idea is to have a lot of ideas." —Dr. Linus Pauling

▶ Know the Rules and When to Break Them
▶ The Meeting: A Team Process
▶ Brainstorming
▶ Problem Solving
▶ Action Plans
▶ Assumptions
▶ Innovation
▶ Teambuilding Foundations

Know the Rules and When to Break Them

Teams develop, refine, create, and solve. Team processes vary, but some of the basics, such as brainstorming and standard problem-solving steps, will create avenues for some of your team's most creative thinking. The benefit of having processes in place is that when the routine breaks or the emergency hits, you are not starting from square one. Your team is experienced in problem-solving methods and has learned to work through challenges together. At the heart of your success in using any tried-and-true method, though, is an openness to adapting those processes to suit your needs or allow for a team member's creative vision.

The Meeting: A Team Process

The meeting is the most common and often underestimated team action. Every staff meeting is, in essence, a teambuilding activity. Who speaks? Who listens? Who hides? Who controls? Who follows through? By putting the reality of teambuilding into context, you can take small measures that yield big results.

Some organizations have weekly or daily meetings to hit the ground running. This method gives credence to the value of everyone hearing the same message at the same time, the necessary interactions and information sharing, the need to jointly solve a problem (or two). Some industries are known for morning meetings within particular departments to ensure clear direction for the day. Other meetings may involve just two people or representatives from different departments. Each of these is an opportunity for team members to interact with, learn from, and support one another.

The more complex the organization, the more bogged down in meetings it may become. Keep in mind when calling a meeting that everyone attending could be doing something else. Most people are juggling too much throughout the day, and every interaction supplants another. Ensure that meetings are meaningful and necessary; clearly communicate the topic and its importance.

The challenge, once you have everyone in the room and a realistic agenda, is keeping everyone on point and eliciting viable contributions from all. Firmly refocus participants who come with their own agendas. Make room for their topics, if appropriate, or suggest a better time. If you find you're getting input from the quick one, the witty one, and the powerhouse, but your thoughtful quiet types don't seem to participate, find a way to include them. Don't miss the opportunity to hear their thoughts because you think they should learn to jump in and shout over. If you have an environment in which only the loud thrive, your team is not accessing everyone's creativity, and you will have members feeling like outsiders. Encourage quiet members to contribute, and bring the focus back to them after interruptions.

Figure 3.1: **THE ON-POINT FACILITATOR**

Facile facilitators understand how to run meetings and facilitate think-sessions that draw on the creativity of all team members. An astute facilitator knows when a meeting's structure is working and when it's time to shake things up.

Are team members operating in small, targeted niches? Have team members swap focus; for instance, have your accountant throw out publicity ideas. Sometimes the answers or starting points for inventive solutions may come from people who don't know that their idea sounds crazy or can't be done. Sometimes the experts overlook the obvious. What ideas might come from someone who is viewing an issue from the outside?

Do:

• Begin on time.

• Clearly state ground rules.

• Ask key questions.

• Keep the discussion focused and moving.

• Encourage participation by all group members.

• Control the flow of the discussion.

• Summarize key issues discussed and decisions made.

• End on time.

Do not:

- Let one or two group members dominate.

- Ignore those who do not speak up.

- Mistake silence for consent.

- Embarrass group members.

- Dominate the discussion by emphasizing your own opinions and/or suggestions.

Stop to refocus the team when:

- One individual monopolizes the discussion and tries to bulldoze his/her choices.

- Someone goes off on a tangent. (Acknowledge the importance of issues raised, and state a better time to address them.)

Restore balance when:

- One person cuts off another's comment.

- One individual says nothing.

QUICK Tip

Involve every aspect of the business: We had a long-standing relationship with Montclair State University's chemistry department, hiring interns over the course of the years and often eventually hiring many of them as full-time Research and Development (R&D) staff.

Staff meetings involved everyone and routinely took place at a breakfast or lunch or, frankly, any time that we needed to delve into a project (frequently) or solve a challenge. Our interns were, at first, quite shy about expressing opinions, but soon realized that they were expected to weigh in and learn about a project by analyzing it from different angles: marketing, sales, purchasing, advertising—not just the technical development of the formulations. How does the consumer respond to the product—ease of use, fulfillment of expectation, scent, feel, etc.?

We brought the technical personnel to listen to market research studies that I conducted one-on-one. They sat behind the two-way mirror and listened as respondents reacted to the product's concept, and then again when the respondent returned to tell us (three weeks later) just what they thought of how the product worked. For the first time, these R&D interns not only worked on the formulations, but also heard what real people thought about using them. University lectures and labs aside, chemistry became a living, breathing animal that they were elbow deep in creating!

—Betty Jagoda Murphy, cofounder ReGenesis LLC

Diversity leads to innovation: Consensus building is critical to a well-functioning team; however, a team in which all ideas are accepted without question or debate will not break new ground. While agreement is gratifying, healthy debate spurs teams to delve more deeply into a problem and search for more creative solutions.

Groupthink may result from team members not wanting to "rock the boat," being concerned with being liked, a persistent desire to "move on" (to feel a quick sense of accomplishment or get to the next item, which may be an early lunch), or a belief that troublemakers don't get ahead. In some cases, the message (subtle or not so subtle) has been "don't rock the boat." Managers can cause groupthink by being intolerant of dissent, rushing to outcomes, rewarding "yes-ers," or offering so much praise and encouragement that the group underestimates the seriousness of potential problems or an appreciation of unique or carefully thought-out solutions.

The advantage of a team is that it is a mesh of personality types, talents, and experiences. While the differences present challenges, they also present a wide array of solutions. Someone who is a natural debater might be able to see things from many angles, but it takes a negotiator to bring them all together. The idealist and the realist may play some ideological tug of war, but ultimately, you'll be lucky to have the two working together. The most viable solutions will usually be discovered somewhere between them.

Brainstorming

Brainstorming is a widely used technique for expanding thinking and generating new, different, and potentially breakthrough ideas. The uncensored approach lets ideas flow freely and build on one another, generating a larger pool of ideas than would a more structured one. It has proven so successful because it helps us overcome our preconceived notions and discard our usual approaches to idea generation and problem solving. By allowing a team to build on the ideas of its individual members, brainstorming promotes the belief that no matter how crazy or irrelevant an idea may seem, it may spark an original and worthwhile one no one would otherwise have thought of.

Simply put, brainstorming is a process by which a group or individual tosses out all ideas on a given topic. The individual might work with a brainstorm outline, writing ideas all over the page without any sense of order or priority. For a group, members typically call out ideas as one person, a facilitator or designated scribe, records the ideas on a flip chart or white board as they come. The process is infused with energy as participants trigger one another's ideas.

Brainstorming can be an effective tool for both individual and group problem solving. The steps are essentially the same. It may be used as a stand-alone tool or may be integrated into a larger idea-generating or problem-solving process.

Brainstorming Steps

1. Establish the topic and set parameters.
2. Communicate ground rules.
3. Set a time limit.
4. List all ideas or suggestions as they are made.
5. Encourage creativity.
6. Don't evaluate.
7. Have the group consolidate like ideas and/or categories and eliminate extraneous points.
8. Prioritize.

Now What?

The group has created a list of potential ideas, and, at this point, the group's momentum is rolling. Now is the time to set in motion a plan for implementing actions and solutions, before the other pressing events put your brainstorm items out of mind. Set SMARTER goals and develop action plans.

Post-brainstorming steps to keep your team moving forward:
• Set SMARTER goals
• Develop action plans
• Communicate

Team Activity: Brainstorming

Choose a current problem/concern, and ask your team to brainstorm solutions following the process outlined above.

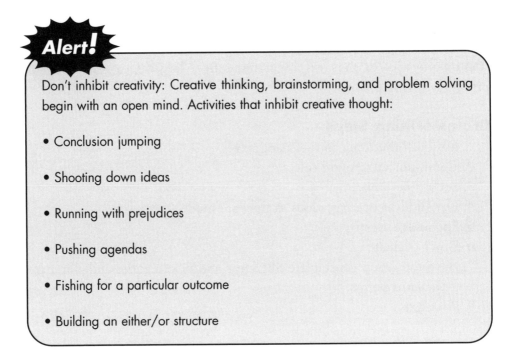

Alert!

Don't inhibit creativity: Creative thinking, brainstorming, and problem solving begin with an open mind. Activities that inhibit creative thought:

- Conclusion jumping

- Shooting down ideas

- Running with prejudices

- Pushing agendas

- Fishing for a particular outcome

- Building an either/or structure

Problem Solving

Problem-solving methods abound. Many techniques kick off creative thinking. Here, we share some basic starting points such as examining assumptions, playing devil's advocate, and the six-step problem-solving method below. These and other methods integrate brainstorming, which is also a highly effective exercise on its own.

Six-Step Problem-Solving Method

(Notice that steps 2 and 3 incorporate brainstorming.)

   1. Identify the problem.
   What are we trying to accomplish or decide?
   Why is it not working as it should?
   How should it work? (State your ideal outcome.)
   As a result of this process, we want _____.
   2. Consider possible causes.
   Brainstorm everything that might be causing the problem.
   Think about: policies, processes, resources, technology, money, and behaviors.

Rank causes according to importance.

3. Identify potential solutions.

Brainstorm possible solutions. (Consider combined solutions.)

Narrow your choices.

Think about what would work: best, most quickly, most economically.

4. Select and plan a solution.

What positive factors are in place now?

What resources exist?

Develop a step-by-step action plan.

Communicate with everyone affected by the plan. Assign responsibilities.

5. Implement the solution.

Follow the plan!

Monitor events.

6. Evaluate.

Was the solution as effective as anticipated? Why? Why not?

What's the team's post-assessment of its reaction/response/resolution?

QUICK Tip

Informal polling: One way to get everyone's input is to put it out to the team, or company, all at once in the form of a posted sign, email, or intranet post. Be clear about where ideas should be submitted. Advantages to this method include getting a broader scope of input than you might otherwise receive and giving people a chance to think through the issue in their own time. Someone could have an "aha" moment that wouldn't have come during the pressure of a time-framed, structured meeting. This method gets people thinking on their own and springing into informal discussions.

Which is better? The structured problem-solving or brainstorm process or the public forum? Each has its place and the use of different methods keeps thinking fresh. The two can also be combined.

Team Activity: The Wooden Dowel

This is a fairly simple exercise that involves six to ten people and a very light, four-foot wooden dowel. The purpose is to illustrate communication and coordination within teams.

Objective: Each team is to lower the wooden dowel to the ground—together.

Instructions:

1. Show the final position that you want their hands and the dowel to be in at the conclusion: right-hand pinky on the ground, dowel balanced across the team's index fingers. Then ask participants to stand shoulder-to-shoulder in two lines facing each other.

2. Instruct them to hold their right arm and hand straight out, turned vertically so that their palms face left and the side of their index finger is on top.

3. Give the following simple ground rules:

   • You cannot place any pressure on top of the stick at any time.

   • If anyone loses contact with the stick the group starts again from the original position.

   • The exercise is complete when everyone's hand is down to the floor.

   • Give a time limit. (I usually give about three minutes to complete the task.)

4. Place the dowel on top of each outstretched hand...on top of the index finger and gently apply downward pressure once everyone is making contact.

5. Make sure that no one has a finger or thumb on top of the dowel and that all participants are making contact with the dowel.

6. Say, "Go" and release your pressure on the dowel.

Process: The dowel immediately moves upward! Each participant is chasing the dowel in the opposite direction that they were instructed to go. Surprise and great laughter ensue.

Participants will usually start speaking up: "Hold it—why are we going this way?" They start to tell each other to lower the stick—all the time they are themselves pressing upward. The dowel goes wildly up until the shorter participants can no longer stay in contact. I then restart the group with a reminder that the objective was to take the dowel to the floor—not the ceiling. I jokingly give them reminders of the difference. That's the floor. That's the ceiling. Slipping off the dowel makes the group start again from the beginning—which builds more frustration.

The second go-around is usually no better than the first as the group begins to get the hang of it. Most times the dowel goes back up or begins to "pitch and yaw," which again makes participants come off contact. I tell them that this is a very light wooden dowel—you just need to lower it together to the floor. Each time I start them over I put downward pressure on the dowel—by the second or third time the group begins to anticipate this, and they start to prepare each other for it.

My favorite group phenomenon occurs when the dowel goes neither up nor down after I release it. The participants are so focused on keeping contact that the group becomes paralyzed. No one person wants to be the person to come off contact—so they don't take risks. I pause the activity to give the group a couple of minutes to discuss their behavior and make a new strategy.

New ideas come from the conversation. Some groups go to an extreme and place all hands near the center on the dowel. This seems right until they lose balance—not only on the dowel but as a group when they each have to reach to the center. The most innovative groups question the "standing" starting point of the exercise. They notice that it's hard to make the switch from standing to the kneeling position that is required to make the last move to the floor and keep in contact with the dowel. So they ask if they can start from a kneeling position. I generally approve this as I feel that the group is learning and questioning some unspoken rules.

The group succeeds when:

• A coach helps the group verbally to make downward movement.

• They reduce the contact points on the stick. They join hands and form small sub teams of two or three people.

• When they make contact with each other (nonverbal communication) they have a better sense of when their partners are moving (another great debrief point).

The teams almost always succeed—in fact I make sure they do in that I don't call them out if someone comes off the stick on the third or fourth try.

The debrief focuses on:

• What happened at the beginning?

• Who was moving the stick up?

• What was the innovative moment?

• Who had the breakthrough strategy?

• Who emerged as the leader?

• Who played the role of the coach?

• How did you feel when you came off the stick?

The tough question is near the end when I ask, "Can you tell me with 100 percent accuracy that everyone on your team maintained contact on the successful run?" Most sheepishly shake their heads. In most cases someone has come off contact and does not want to ruin the successful attempt. I equate that with quality in the workplace. Does quality matter and how can you ensure that team members feel it's okay to point out defects—before the product goes to market?

For me this is a fun and very robust team activity with lots of potential applications and versions—all using a simple wooden dowel.

—Contributed by Dino Signore, program manager for The Edward Lowe Foundation, MI, edwardlowe.org and principal owner of the Sherpa Group consulting firm

Team Activity: Devil's Advocate

Playing devil's advocate can be a useful exercise but should not be overused or become a habit that translates into a perpetual negative response that is no longer useful. Use this technique to look at a problem from different viewpoints. This can be especially helpful when trying to solve problems that involve other workgroups or divisions. By anticipating the thinking or position of another group you are able to develop more productive suggestions and strategies.

Step 1: Divide the team to examine the problem from three points of view. These may be those of people with different interests who are connected to your business, such as customer, advertiser, and vendor; or developer, end user, investor; or simply viewpoints of optimist, pessimist, and realist. If you have a small group of three, let each person take one position. For larger groups, break into groups of three, each representing one position.

Step 2: Brainstorm what you think each person or group would say about the problem. What positions would they take?

Step 3: Note the validity of the opposing points of view and identify any similarities. Work to reduce or eliminate the anticipated objections others may have.

This should provide you with clarity about the ways in which others see the situation and help troubleshoot any potential conflicts. This information will help your team answer objections and create solutions that should have broad-spectrum appeal and acceptance.

Action Plans

Another mainstay of team process is the action plan. For every goal, new idea, or problem-solving plan, someone needs to take action. Action plans ensure that everyone knows what his or her responsibility is. When functioning as a group, some people may have a tendency to assume someone else must be taking care of an item that was raised, an item that inevitably falls through the cracks. A useful action plan states who is doing what, by when, and with what resources.

Everyone who has a stake in a plan's success should be involved in the creation and evolution of the action plan. Once a team identifies a problem's resolution, assigning tasks to bring that resolution home is best done in a team environment. Immediately create an assignment list for each team member involved. Establish checkpoints and deadlines to ensure your team's success, inventory necessary resources, and connect with others whose contributions may be tangential or small but critical.

Team Activity: Action Planning

Think of a company goal or goals that you want your team to achieve. Use the following formats to take your team through the process of making that goal a reality.

Step 1:

Goals
Identify one or more goals.

Activities to Achieve Goals
What activities are necessary to achieve each goal?

Step 2:

Now, get down to details.

Tasks _____

Expected Outcomes _____

Responsible Party _____

Target Date _____

Resources _____

Status _____

Step 3: Is the team lacking in resources, information, or expertise to get the job done? Make a plan and put someone in charge of following through.

Some alternative forms of action planning could be games—just remember to use the core values and principles that guided the development of the goals and action plans as the basis for the games, as well:

• Create a card game with department or company-specific case studies, and assign teams to solve them and then discuss with the larger group.

• Create a board game that focuses on profit drivers and detractors.

• Create a board game that requires teams to arrive at solutions to nagging or emergent problems.

• Model a game after one of the popular quiz shows or board games to introduce a new initiative or culture change.

Assumptions

We all carry our assumptions with us; some of us have more than others. What are your assumptions about assumptions? The number one assumption check: do you assume that coming to the table with assumptions is always a *bad* thing? Be careful not to confuse your assumptions with ultimate reality, but don't try to force them out of your head either. Assumptions are generally bad only when they are used to jump to conclusions or as truths that should not be challenged.

Assumptions are natural, and those unexpressed will likely be more limiting than those openly examined. You might assume an idea will never fly, so you don't say it. You might assume that so-and-so will never approve, so you only halfheartedly share the idea because it's a waste of time anyway, isn't it? If someone suggests a project that you think would be world-class, but you assume the expense will be too high, you will shoot down the idea instead of exploring cost-cutting solutions, avenues for revenue, funding, or areas where other costs might easily be curtailed to accommodate. The assumption might not even be true at all; an available funding source may have been overlooked.

Examining team member assumptions is a great starting point for raising questions or simply clearing the mind of preconceived notions or airing differences up front. Assumptions are valuable resources for information and pertinent questions. We might have assumptions hiding in our own minds that seem so self-evident and unquestionable that we don't even flesh them out and consider they might not be as real as we think. We might even call them beliefs. Of course, even more confusing is being on a team in which members are guided by beliefs and assumptions that are not discussed. Treading only the surface of issues will always create limitations for the team.

By strengthening your team's ability to recognize and clarify assumptions, you prepare them not only to work more effectively together, but arm them to address potential client/customer assumptions and objections.

Team Activity: Assuming Assumptions Can Be Useful

Ask each member to list assumptions relating to an upcoming project or proposed idea.

Give ten minutes to write out assumption lists. Have team members share their assumptions, writing each on a flip chart or presentation screen. Screen out repeats as you write, but mark them to demonstrate the scope of each.

Step 1: Choose a few key assumptions, even some obvious ones (such as, "this project is difficult; it will take some time to complete"), and have team members answer the following questions within the group.

On what facts/information are these assumptions based? (This question can lead to interesting revelations from other team members. Guide the discussion, but don't rush it.)

- How will these assumptions limit my ability to creatively design/market/discuss the matter at hand?

- Has a negative past experience shaped these assumptions?

- What can I learn from that experience that I can apply here?

- Are these assumptions likely to be shared by others of my age/cultural/financial status?

- Are these assumptions held by other team members?

Step 2: The assumption may have been debunked by this stage. If not, and it raises concerns, reframe the "assumption" as a problem and work as a team to brainstorm possible solutions, clearly stating actions to be taken. The two-column think pad below is useful for laying out solutions to any potential problems.

Potential Problems _____

_____

Solutions/Actions _____

_____

Innovation

We will only give a cursory introduction to innovation here because we talk about it in later chapters, especially those on change and taking stock (of where your business is and where it can go). But we introduce the ideas here because change and innovation are part of every creative process and taking stock is not only a major process, but is incorporated (on a small scale) into the daily functioning of a creatively energized team. No matter what your problem-solving methods, you are looking for innovative ideas and solutions.

Encourage creativity to go beyond problem solving, as well. One good activity to give your team is brainstorming possible improvements to a product, system, or process that is already working. Even if your sales are strong, have your team brainstorm ways to make them soar. You may have a team member who is aware of low or no-cost Internet marketing solutions that will enhance your visibility. Often, the creative "dump" without pressure, a deadline, or an immediate need to change or correct course yields dynamic results.

Ask team members to imagine the next big innovation in your industry. You never know where that spark of an idea might lead. Then, look at a possible innovation on the distant horizon, one that might be ten or twenty years away. Let ideas be outrageous; you never know. If nothing useful comes out of it, you have still gotten them thinking creatively, along innovative lines and, hopefully, having some productive fun.

QUICK Tip

Thinking outside of the box: The debate raged for decades in the meeting rooms of swimsuit designers. Imagine the breakout thinking session when the first company decided to create the first chest-revealing men's swimsuit in 1932. The "topper" was clearly a compromise between the bold and cautious, sold with a detachable zippered-on top. Many men who unzipped and went bottoms-only were arrested for indecent exposure.

—Source: swimsuit-style.com

Team Activity: Alternative Scenarios

Scenarios are qualitatively different descriptions of plausible futures. They can give you a deeper understanding of potential environments in which you might have to operate and what you may need to do in the present. Scenario analysis helps you to identify what environmental factors to monitor over time, so that when the environment shifts, you can recognize where it is shifting to.

Thinking through several scenarios is a less risky, more conservative approach to planning than relying on single forecasts and trend analyses. It can thus free up management to take more innovative actions.

Scenarios are developed specifically for a particular problem. To begin developing scenarios:

1. State the specific decision that needs to be made.

2. Identify the major environmental forces that impact on the decision. For example, suppose you need to decide how to invest R&D funds in order to be positioned for opportunities that might emerge by the year 2010. The major environmental forces might include social values, economic growth worldwide, and international trade access (tariffs, etc.).

3. Build four scenarios based on principal forces. To do this, use information available to you to identify four plausible and qualitatively different possibilities for each force. Assemble the alternatives for each force into internally consistent "stories," with both a narrative and a table of forces. Build your scenarios around these forces. For instance, a Midwestern bank used scenarios to stimulate new ideas for maintaining a strong consumer-lending business in upcoming deregulation. Scenario story lines emerged for "at present," "heated," "belt tightening," and "isolation."

4. With the scenarios in hand, identify business opportunities within each scenario.

5. Examine the links and synergies of opportunities across the range of scenarios. This would help you to formulate a more realistic strategy for investment.

—Contributed by William C. Miller, author of *Flash of Brilliance: Inspiring Creativity Where You Work* and founder and president, Global Creativity Corporation, www.globalcreativitycorp.com

Teambuilding Foundations

Team leaders set foundations and maintain a tone throughout the working relationship with the team; they should maintain this tone in small ways throughout the teambuilding process, whether it's a teambuilding exercise or a "think session." Many teambuilding activities that seem like fun and games have a serious purpose and benefit. Often just showing your team that you value them enough to take the time to work on their team skills is in and of itself a motivator.

When conducting a teambuilding activity, start by answering the ever-important WIFM question, the question on everyone's mind: What's in It For Me? Connect the dots from what they're doing to the value of what they will gain once the activity and camaraderie are over. You may not have to do this every time, and some exercises may benefit from not stating objectives up front, but keep in mind that exercises work best when you have some buy-in.

Other ways to create buy-in are to break the ice with some humor or, if an exercise is particularly silly-sounding, demonstration. Show that you're not above playing along. Laugh at yourself and allow yourself to be laughed with, even laughed at. Any team exercise, even a serious one created to produce specific outcomes, can be introduced in a lighthearted way.

If times are particularly stressful, if your team is heavily burdened, share a little something of your story. Let them know you've been there, and you respect how challenging their tasks/jobs are and that you know how hard they've been working. Let them know how much you respect their talents, perseverance, or creativity.

As you continue through a process or session, stay tuned in to your group. Have they hit a wall? Are they dozing? Do they look like they're in pain? If you notice your team is overly stressed, stop and conduct a breathing exercise. It doesn't have to be anything formal, just a reminder and some deep breaths together. Maybe a get-up-and-stretch break is needed, too. Lead stretches, do a stretch free-for-all, but participate so others will feel more comfortable joining in.

Team Activity: The Ad Hoc Book Club

Select a newly released book relating to your business or business development and pull together your team. Depending on the size of your company, this could be your "team of the whole," your management team, or cross-functional representatives. Determine a realistic time frame for everyone to read the selection. Ask each person to develop one or more discussion questions that explore the concepts introduced and suggest that they tie them to your business and your team as a way to initiate discussion. Set a time and date for the book talk. Often, discussions generated by a catalyst, such as reading the same book, follow tangents to exciting ideas.

Team Activity: Create-Your-Own

Divide a larger group into smaller groups of four or five. Give groups fifteen to twenty minutes to come up with a challenging small-group activity. The activity should be one that the group believes it can do better than any other group. Then all groups come together and take turns to present their activity. No equipment is necessary, but tossing in a few objects for optional use could make for interesting outcomes.

Groups earn points if:

• No other group can beat them at their activity (+2)

• They can successfully perform another group's activity (+1)

This exercise requires all elements of team work, including creativity, communication, trust, problem solving, and time management. Encourage creative out-of-the-box thinking (e.g., singing, dancing, joke telling, non-verbal, as well as physical or mental challenges).

—Adapted from *Create Your Own Team Task* by James Neill, researcher, lecturer, adventurer of the mind and planet, www.wilderdom.com

Break-taking: Sometimes, stopping is part of the process. Don't underestimate the power of a break to refresh and recharge. If the meeting is getting bogged down, a break might be in order. Sometimes we're so busy we literally don't even have time to think. Ideas often come in moments of relaxation, coming to us as soon as we stop thinking—that great idea that bubbles up in the shower, the name you couldn't remember that pops in your head as soon as you completely give up on remembering.

Your team members who plod through the day without a break could easily burn out. Encourage short breaks in the action: for thinking, not thinking, fresh air, stretching, fun, meditating, or dart throwing. In a long, stressful day, give a moment for people to do something small and good for themselves. If it seems that everyone has to drive full force every second of every day, working through lunch and dinner, you will have a hard time maintaining motivation. You'll have a team of overworked people who feel mechanized.

Celebrate the natural breaks between projects or after a stressful time. Show your appreciation and let the team celebrate completion, blow off steam, and, heck, even have some fun. Teams that build memories and get to know each other in "real life-outside-the-office" situations add to trust and an overall good feeling about the team. The company picnic; the outing to say, "thanks for your hard work and dedication;" these small things have a big impact.

QUICK Tip

Have a wrap-up party: Generally, our workflow is very smooth. But we had a very difficult month last year. Not only were we extremely busy, not only did we have staff in and out of the office on vacations and seminars, not only did the projects morph and complicate themselves as if they were infecting each other, but we also somehow distilled all the problems we might expect to have in a year into that one month. Impossible requests and frustrated clients bumping up against overstressed staff. As morale began to sink in the office I promised a wrap-up celebration at the end of the month when most of the projects would be completed. We asked everyone to keep track of all their grievances in a creative way. Writing them on a piece of paper was okay, but writing them on a large marshmallow was better! Putting that piece of paper into a peashooter or egg roll was also acceptable. Labeling a dart with the offending situation or action was encouraged. Taping their written grievance to a peg suitable for pounding worked, too. On the appointed day we put on party hats, filled glasses with champagne, and trooped outside to a conveniently placed metal wheelbarrow. We built a fire and blew noisemakers while we toasted the marshmallows, burned the offending actions, used the peashooter to send our now historical problems to the flames, and, in general, destroyed all the bad karma from the month.

—Patricia May, president and CEO, Precision Language Services, Lakeville, MN, www.precisionlanguage.com

Chapter  4

Communication

"People have been known to achieve more as a result of working with others than against them." —Dr. Allan Fromme

- ▶ How Important Is Communication?
- ▶ Information Sharing
- ▶ Clarity
- ▶ Question-Friendly Environments
- ▶ Listening
- ▶ Nothing Personal
- ▶ Follow-Through
- ▶ Means of Communication

How Important Is Communication?

Clear, ongoing communication is the most essential factor in creating and sustaining team achievement. As a leader, a communication culture begins with you. Those who are part of your team want to know what you expect, how you want it done, and when. Most people leave their crystal balls at home; yet, they are called upon regularly to read minds. Creating a flow of clear, open, productive communication requires not only working on fundamentals, but also a careful look at ourselves and our own communication styles.

Shared understanding, from the smallest communication to the grandest goal, is essential for team success. We all know how easily miscommunications occur and that they can have wide-reaching implications that affect the success of any project or business. The missed, mixed, muddled messages; the missed points, lost opportunities, and hours spent needlessly working in wrong directions that could have been avoided (then more hours to get back in the right direction) cost time, money, and trust.

Clear communication:

- Builds trust
- Avoids misunderstandings
- Inspires commitment
- Discovers untapped potential
- Increases comfort with change
- Curbs damaging rumors
- Reduces stress
- Instructs
- Inspires

Incorrect interpretations can be caused by signals the speaker gives (intentionally or unintentionally), the listener's beliefs or preconceived notions, tone of voice (or perceived tone of voice), personal prejudices, insecurities, or biases. Think of a simple question, like "Are you finished with the new design yet?" The person being asked might perceive judgment or be dealing with his or her own issues about not being finished yet, when the question might have simply been framed that way out of anticipation or coincidence. The one who asked the question might be perplexed by a hostile reply; the one feeling "questioned" would say the other one started the conflict.

Figure 4.1: **KNOW YOUR AUDIENCE**

Who is your audience? Whether writing or speaking, knowing your audience helps you tailor your message for the greatest impact. No one will buy in, join in, build on our ideas, or take part in the successful outcome we desire if our messages are unclear or leave listeners/readers wondering why they should care and what relation the message has to what they are trying to accomplish.

Often, when we try to communicate more clearly, we run what we write or say through a filter that asks, "Does this make sense?" The problem with that question is that it implies "to me?" If it makes sense in your own mind, you may be impatient with someone who doesn't understand. Ask: "Would it make sense to _____?" Focus on your audience. Messages should be clear and directed.

What do you know about your audience?

Level of Information:

• How familiar is your listener/reader with the topic?

• How much of the main message should you share?

• How much background information will be helpful?

Style:

• Do you know your listener's/reader's attitudes toward the topic? Toward you?

• What barriers or problems might occur?

• What can you do to make this conversation/correspondence positive for the other person?

Direction:

• What action do you want the listener/reader to take?

• What information does the listener/reader need in order to carry out the request?

Information Sharing

"Information is power" is the mantra of those who hoard it. The real power, in fact, comes from shared information. By sharing facts and insights with team members, you expand the brainpower devoted to the problem at hand. Working teams communicate concerns, deadlines, changes, and facts.

Sharing knowledge and information is essential to team success. Information sharing should be part of your organization's overall strategic plan. In fact, be sure to include in your performance evaluation process a rating of how openly and proficiently team members share information.

Some team members are reluctant to share information because they believe they increase their value by being the only one who knows where or how or has access to certain resources. That reluctance, however, hurts the team, holding it back from optimal performance for the sake of personal ego. Others do not believe their contributions will be valued or are valuable. Help them recognize that even a minor suggestion can have a major impact. Still others are looking for a "free ride." Every team has those who coast, and every team member knows who they are. The coaster is detrimental to the team in many ways. First, causing factions of "I don't want to work with him/her" detracts from the goal. Second, team members who don't contribute deprive the team of the benefit of their knowledge or "take" on a given situation.

Sources and Storage

Information abounds, especially on the superhighway. As members of a team acquire information, they should be careful to collect sources as they go. With so much available information, a team might want to determine "trustworthy" sources and have a system for evaluating and approving new ones. The system should be simple and direct, not one in which good information gets bogged down or people limit resources to avoid a bottleneck.

Also, information will do no good if it ends up on the bottom of a paper pile or in a poorly-marked file on one person's computer. Create a knowledge base for data collected over time, ideally with systems for updating and refining. The team must have clear, workable systems for storage and retrieval.

Clarity

Clarity is an exercise for both the speaker and the listener. Keep in mind how easy it is to miss giving or comprehending critical information when you are rushing. Sometimes, you may assume people know more than they do. This, of course, is true for others, too. Be as vigilant as you can in both giving clear messages and receiving them.

You know the package has to be there tomorrow. You stress the urgency of sending it out today. The package is sent out today—regular mail. If you want it sent by overnight mail, say so. Do not assume that the listener can read your thoughts. Be clear. Be thorough. Finish your thoughts. If you don't, the listener will use his or her best guess to finish them for you.

As a result of time constraints or habit, we often give direction or instruction without explaining the rationale behind it. Knowing the big picture makes the details clearer. Clarity is the backbone of a team; sure, you know what's going on, but you're part of a team. Everyone has to be clear on the plan. The more we can explain, the more we can expect clear understanding and good decision-making.

We all know that some people are easier to communicate with than others. Have you ever said, "He never listens. Why bother?" Choosing not to communicate with someone because that person seems to be a poor communicator leaves you a poor communicator, too, doubling your odds of a breakdown in team process. If someone is on your team or affects it, find a way to communicate.

Finding the Right Method

Part of clarity is conveying important information in different ways, understanding that not everyone processes in the same way. Some people find it easier to process information verbally and have difficulty wading through long emails, while others absorb best what they can see in writing. Additionally, we respond to ideas that are framed in specific ways. People will often give clues to how they process in subtleties of wording.

On the next page are some examples of different expressions of the same ideas by people with various processing strengths. (While we all "get" the meaning and can translate quickly to our own "language" without even noticing, we might feel more at home with phrases that speak directly to us.)

- The tactile person: Can you get your arms around this problem?
- The visual person: How do you see it?
- The auditory person: How does that sound to you?

What's the answer with a growing team? Since tapping into everyone's strongest processing methods is impractical, provide important information from several angles, if possible. For instance, provide important announcements verbally, but back them up with an email or post in a public area. It is feasible, too, to note the processing styles of those closest to you and work with them the best you can and to be open with everyone about yours. Tell people when a passing comment isn't enough and what you need in writing, even informally.

QUICK Tip

The ABCs of clear communication: Sending a clear message (written or verbal) means keeping your communications as simple as ABC: Accurate, Brief, and Clear.

Accurate: Communicate a clear objective or goal.

Brief: Succinctly state what actions or input you need.

Clear: Tailor your message to be clear to the receiver.

See it from both sides: Early in my career, I directed a newly-created adult learning center. I reported to Harry Linkin, the director of Adult Education for the regional school district. Two people reported to me; dozens reported to Harry. Often, when walking to or from meetings or a quick lunch, I would offer ideas and suggestions. Harry would reply by asking me to write him a note (pre-email). I always felt a little put out, a little taken advantage of; it seemed controlling. He heard; he understood; yet, he needed it in writing. As the learning center grew and my staff went from three to twelve instructors and counselors, I'd find when walking from one room to another that staff members assailed me with ideas and problems. Knowing I couldn't possibly keep it all in mind while focusing on the tasks at hand, I found myself saying, "Please, write it down," smiling inwardly at how I had misjudged Harry's intention." —Harriet Diamond

Language

Language—so simple, so complex, so powerful. Language differences can be difficult; sensitivity to and awareness of potential problems are mandatory for clear communication. Even when we're speaking the same language, we don't always "speak the same language." Understanding the context often clarifies meaning. In cross-cultural circumstances, remember that one word might have a very different meaning or connotation in another language. Even in English, words have multiple meanings, and the same word can carry a different meaning, depending on tone (which is easily misperceived) or content. Simple phrases can conjure very different intentions: Think of the phrase, "Can I see you in my office?"

Are you aware of words that trip off your negative responses or cause you to shut down? Most of us have them. Keep in mind that many people who use those "hot button" words do not know your particular sensitivity and may mean them differently than you imagine. For instance, a team member may say your idea has "some merit," and you put the emphasis on "some," feeling belittled, while a compliment and readiness to consider your idea is the actual intent. You might say a team member has "new age" notions while that person holds a notion of "new agers" as "flakes." In your mind, it was a compliment and showed appreciation for a much-needed viewpoint. Everyone has some little sensitivity. Reality checks and open, nondefensive communication are the best strategies for working well together and getting beyond the sticking points we've all accumulated over time.

Shades of Meaning

People may say…	When they mean…
Yes/No	Maybe
Maybe	Probably not
As soon as possible	Eventually
Later	Much, much later (if ever)
Yes (or nod)	I hear you; I acknowledge that you think so

Unclear expectations, poor communication, and sometimes just plain miscommunication in the press of the day can disturb the equilibrium in your work environment. Fix it fast, and move on.

QUICK Tip

A positive spin: One way to buffer a message and excise the negative impact is to find different ways of saying "no" and "I don't know." We can create a more positive message by using phrases like:

• "I'm sorry I can't get to that this morning, but I'll get back to you before the end of the day."

• "As soon as I finish this (project, research, report, item, brochure), you are my top priority."

• "I have a concern about…"

• "I believe I need to let you know…"

• "I'd like us to discuss…"

- "I have some thoughts about…"

- "I wish I could, but here is what I can do…"

- "Let me explain what I know…"

- "It was my impression that…"

Question-Friendly Environments

Teams that run smoothly create question-friendly environments. When questions are greeted with impatience, the questioner retreats, decides to "figure it out," "punt," or just "forget it." All of these solutions are open to dire consequences. Even "figure it out," which may be empowering and positive, becomes a negative when the team member has less than enough or inaccurate information on which to base his or her "figuring."

If you have limited time (which you do), plan time for staff or team questions. Set aside a brief time in your hectic schedule to be available to answer questions that, when unanswered, slow others down. If you are one who deals with issues as they come at you, give brief, to-the-point answers or refer the questioner to the appropriate person or resource and move on.

There are those who need answers but shy away from asking because the one whom they must ask is a bit too detailed in his or her responses. The simple answer becomes a lecture, a lengthy anecdote, or an entirely new conversation. Notice your style. If you recognize yourself in this one, work on streamlining.

You also benefit from taking time to ask questions of those on your team. Should you find that your questions are greeted with abrupt responses or rolled eyes, consider your timing. Some people react to the untimely question as though it's a cannon, interrupting their thoughts and work rhythm. The best approach is to begin with a brief stage-setter: Do you have time to answer a few questions about XYZ? I'm having some trouble tracking down that information we discussed; when you have minute, can we talk? I'm interested in your progress on this. When would you have time to fill me in? These questions are respectful of your team members' time and ensure that you'll receive undivided attention when you do get to ask your specific questions.

All questions are not equal. They do not create the same ambiance, elicit the same information, or serve the same purpose. Following are three types of questions: open, closed, and summary.

Closed Questions: Closed questions require a one-word response, such as a simple "yes" or "no," and typically do not allow the person questioned to elaborate. These questions work when you want to confirm facts or information and move on.

Most closed questions begin with:

Do you...?	Can you...?
How many...?	Are you...?
Will you...?	Did you...?

Open Questions: Open questions require a more detailed response. This type of question allows one to probe for understanding, clarify, and seek input.

Open questions encourage dialogue and often begin with:

What...?	Tell me...
Who...?	Show me...
Why...?	Explain...
When...?	Describe...
How do you...?	

Summary Questions: Summary questions are key for any communication. The more people participating, the greater the opportunity for misunderstanding. Summary questions assess the listener's or participant's understanding of information, directions, or decisions.

Listening

Listening is the most valuable communication tool. Only through listening can we learn facts, issues, and others' points of view. Encourage everyone's participation.

A supportive environment that encourages new ideas and creativity enhances teamwork. A repressive or competitive environment stifles team spirit and breeds mistrust.

When someone is talking, focus. Show that you are listening through receptive body language and responses. How often have you muttered for someone to go on, saying "I'm listening" as you were reading your email, checking phone messages, signing papers, surfing the Web, or planning your afternoon, only to realize later you had no idea what had been said? Listen.

If you cannot listen at a given time, say so and arrange for a time when you can pay attention to the person speaking. Listening requires attention. Indicate how much time you have now; say when you will have more. However, take a quick assessment of how urgent the message is. It might save you time in the end to listen.

Honing your listening skills demonstrates your interest in others and their input. When people feel no one is listening, they start to wonder "Why bother?"

Demonstrate listening by:
- Maintaining eye contact
- Giving nonverbal cues
- Nodding, leaning toward the speaker
- Asking open questions
- Responding when appropriate
- Encouraging the speaker by using words such as: "yes," "I see," and "go on"
- Using pauses deliberately
- Not interrupting
- Not completing the speaker's sentences
- Summarizing

Focus on the Speaker

We all know that outward signs of listening are not foolproof. Many people show these signs to look as though they're listening; the most important thing you can do to improve your listening is to focus.

Staying focused means clearing a mental space and paying full attention to the message.

1. Focus your mind.
2. Monitor yourself; recognize when your concentration has strayed; refocus.
3. Confirm. Check your understanding through questioning and paraphrasing.

Listening requires cutting down on external and internal distractions. Beyond outside distractions are internal ones, such as thinking about one of the trillion other things on your mind or thinking about your response instead of listening. Still, other distractions to listening are those that come from our own internal barriers. What barriers might prevent understanding?

Judging, stereotyping, interrupting, and discomfort over status and role differences are all internal barriers that can be overcome by self-awareness and patient practice. If emotional responses are your barrier, slow down. Focus on content, not delivery. Take a moment before responding, and make the effort to find points of agreement. If time constraints are distracting, reschedule. Only you have the power to remove your own barriers.

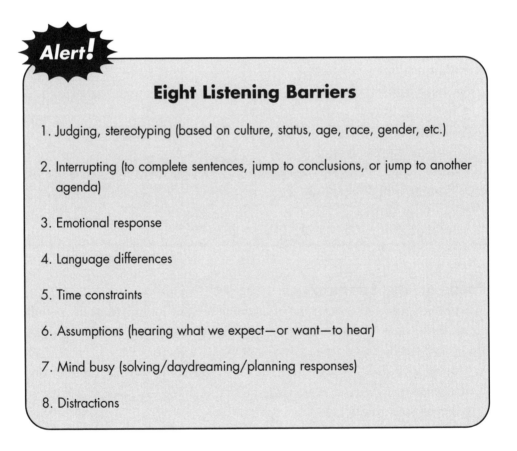

Alert!

Eight Listening Barriers

1. Judging, stereotyping (based on culture, status, age, race, gender, etc.)

2. Interrupting (to complete sentences, jump to conclusions, or jump to another agenda)

3. Emotional response

4. Language differences

5. Time constraints

6. Assumptions (hearing what we expect—or want—to hear)

7. Mind busy (solving/daydreaming/planning responses)

8. Distractions

Leadership Activity: Listening Self-Test

True False

1. I often get bored and daydream instead of listening.

2. I am easily distracted.

3. I tend to interrupt.

4. I often change the subject to suit my own agenda.

5. If I don't understand what was said, I am more likely to smile and nod than ask questions.

6. I avoid eye contact with the speaker.

7. I like to multitask while listening.

8. I tune out the speaker when the message is too complicated.

9. I tune out a speaker whose behavior, voice quality, or appearance bothers me.

10. When asked whether I understand, I answer "Yes," thinking I'll figure it out later if it's important.

What's the score? You know the score. Every time you answered "false," that question is a statement of your listening strengths. "True" shows areas for improvement. Jot down these and other strengths/areas for improvement that you have noticed in yourself and those others may have pointed out to you.

How well do you listen?

Strengths _____

_____

Areas for Improvement _____

_____

Team Activity: Listening

Organize a partner activity. Give very clear instructions: 1) Within each team of two, one partner will speak for six minutes without interruption, answering one or both of the following questions: "What helps me work my best?" and "What gets in the way?" If you think you are through speaking before "time" is called, take a moment, and you'll probably be able to keep going. The listener will make eye contact with the speaker but will give no feedback at all. 2) Once "time" is called, change roles, and the listeners will speak, and the speakers will listen. 3) Now, each speaker will briefly talk about the experience of receiving total, unqualified attention. Once everyone has had a chance, facilitate a discussion about the process of total, unqualified listening. Ask each person to discuss from the perspective of speaker and listener. Ask the question of speakers, "How did you feel?" and chart the answers. 4) Now, lead a discussion about how the lessons learned can be applied to working with others.

QUICK Tip

More Communication Tools

Empathize: Put yourself in the other's shoes. How would you feel in a similar situation?

Mirror: Reflect the speaker's words and feelings to demonstrate understanding.

Paraphrase: Paraphrasing is the act of repeating what someone else has said using your own words. Paraphrasing tells both the speaker and listener whether or not they are on the same page.

Use Examples: Using examples can improve communication with others. Examples help illustrate a topic by providing the listener with the proper context or frame of reference. Examples assist the listener in interpreting the speaker's intent.

Make time to talk: As president of MMI Associates, Inc., a Raleigh, NC, marketing and public relations firm, I knew exercise was important, but my busy schedule did not permit regular trips to the gym. Solution? I decided to take a daily twenty-minute walk around the grounds where my office is located. Accordingly, I stuffed a pair of walking shoes and socks into the back of my car.

Not one to walk alone, I came up with the idea of inviting a different staff member to join me each day. What started out as a spontaneous break for exercise and fresh air soon developed into something more utilitarian—a valuable opportunity to have some one-on-one time with each of my employees. I quickly discovered that my daily walks with employees fostered bonding. My company's account executives tended to share tidbits about both themselves and MMI clients that otherwise might never have been discussed. The company's operations manager welcomed the chance to hash out some tough managerial issues without having to pull me into the back room and have the whole staff worry about what was up. And the writer who normally spent the day alone in the "bat cave" positively glowed with invigoration after our walk-and-talks.

As a result of regular walks with each staff member, I have a better handle on the work ebb and flow in the office and feel more up-to-date on what is happening with my clients. I know my people and my clients better than ever before.

For a coaching and mentoring opportunity, the walk can't be beat. My staff loves to pick my brain, and I enjoy sharing my expertise. I feel free to ask each person the kinds of questions during a walk together that I probably would refrain from asking in the more formal atmosphere of the

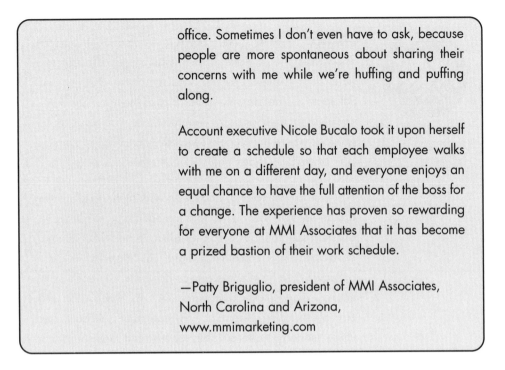

office. Sometimes I don't even have to ask, because people are more spontaneous about sharing their concerns with me while we're huffing and puffing along.

Account executive Nicole Bucalo took it upon herself to create a schedule so that each employee walks with me on a different day, and everyone enjoys an equal chance to have the full attention of the boss for a change. The experience has proven so rewarding for everyone at MMI Associates that it has become a prized bastion of their work schedule.

—Patty Briguglio, president of MMI Associates, North Carolina and Arizona, www.mmimarketing.com

Nothing Personal

Focus on issues, not personalities. Accept work styles that differ from your own. You may work ninety miles an hour and get a week's worth of work done in a day. That's great, but that's not everyone's style. Usually high-powered creative people tend to overlook details, even make mistakes. Working side-by side with a cautious, 40 mph colleague or employee can be just what you need.

Personal differences between the speaker and listener—such as their positions in the organization, cultural backgrounds, and language—may influence understanding. Focusing on issues rather than personalities is always more productive. By addressing issues only, the team can maintain focus and streamline discussions. "He said, she said" debates are time-consuming and counterproductive.

For instance, calling attention to Josh's "negative attitude" will derail your problem-solving session. Asking Josh to play "devil's advocate" will engage him in the discussion and raise issues others might overlook. If Cindi's perpetually missing meetings is causing problems, calling her "lazy," accusing her of "slacking off," or making idle little threats will not change her behavior or transform her into a more active team member. Saying nothing, of course, does nothing. She needs to be told how her behavior affects the team. You might say: "Your role is important, and we need to have you there to share updates and answer questions." "Your input is critical to the team's success." Or, "When you don't show up at meetings, others decide their presence isn't important either; without touching base regularly, our team communication breaks down."

We all have our own communication comfort levels. We can feel put off by styles that seem too abrupt, too obtuse, too slow, too loud, too soft, not enough like our own styles, or too much like ourselves. Stretch beyond your comfort zone. When you encounter a style that grates on you, listen even harder to the message.

Sometimes, team members have had issues with each other in the past, and grudges, large and small, remain. Whatever the original cause, at this point it's *not* business; it's just personal. Move past the history. The future is the team's goal, and helping everyone on the team succeed is essential to *everyone's* success. What are the issues at hand? What are the goals? What does each of these members need from the other? If Ella and Louis are at odds within your team, remind them of the goal and that neither succeeds without the other. If the issue is between you and someone on your team, be the peacemaker and the first to go out of your way with a show of good faith.

As always, watch your words. If you want someone's help, support, empathy, or motivated efforts, respect is the watchword. Making judgments or using condescending tones or language will not inspire, but will instantly disconnect someone from caring about your wants/needs/concerns.

You might think it, but don't say:

"Why didn't she just ask? ...tell?"

"Shouldn't he be smart enough to know?"

"He never listens. Why bother?"

"It doesn't matter anyway."

"How stupid can you be?"

"Whatever."

"It's not rocket science."

"Not the sharpest saw in the shop."

Team Member Activity:
Self-Assessment: Perceptions and Comfort Zones

Be aware of your comfort zones. Ignoring or denying them will not help you move beyond them to create a welcoming atmosphere for those whose styles may be different from your own.

For each number, circle one answer that best describes you.

I am most comfortable with people who:

1)   a. get right to the point

      b. are thoughtful and take time during a discussion

2)   a. share my values, fit right in

      b. bring a new perspective to a problem

3)   a. are self-sufficient

b. are team-oriented

4)   a. don't mind a few laughs on the job

b. stick to the task at hand

5)   a. work quickly—even if everything isn't perfect

b. check and recheck before moving on

6)   a. work within guidelines—no matter what

b. challenge the tried and true

7)   a. question everything

b. follow directions without ever questioning

8)   a. speak plainly

b. use inside jargon

9)   a. need structure

b. prefer no structure

10) a. use good grammar

b. don't always use good grammar

11) a. are at my level in the organization

b. are at a lower level

c. are at an upper level

12) a. are of my own age group

     b. are older than I am

     c. are younger than I am

Okay, now you know. There are no right or wrong answers. The trick is being aware of your thought process and personal biases so you can pull the "breaker switch" before your automatic shut-off engages.

Follow-Through

When you say you will do something, do it. Follow-through is a critical component of communication. The clearest communication is meaningless without it. If items are slipping through the cracks, and your team has more excuses than results, all communication was a waste of time and energy. Team members need to be able to count on one another and team members must understand that someone's word is his or her most important business asset.

If you cannot follow through yourself, follow through by finding someone who can. Confirm, if any doubt exists, that it is all right to hand the item off to someone who can see it through, and communicate that you have passed it along and to whom. Be certain that all expectations, directions, and contact information have been passed along, as well. Once you have agreed to do something, or you know the expectation is that you will, follow-through becomes your responsibility. Check back to ensure that the task went smoothly, as though successful completion is your responsibility—because it is.

Follow Up

Follow through includes following up. If you have a deadline of November 1 and attach a file and hit send on November 1, follow up to ensure that it was received. Good questions include: "Does it look all right?" and "Do you need anything else?" Don't wait to find out post-deadline that your email never arrived or there was a problem with the attachment.

Whose fault is it? Does it matter? Sure, you want to clarify to avoid future problems, but the issue of the moment is the work that needs to be done. Yes, the person who was supposed to receive it could have followed up with you, but if it was your responsibility to get it in, it's also your responsibility to ensure that it did. If you are on the other end, take responsibility there, too. Pop back an email to ensure the sender it was received and attachments looked fine. Whichever end you find yourself on, communicate.

Look beyond your team: Survey the external environment. What is the work environment in which your team must function? How do your team's goals align (or conflict) with the goals of others? For example, another department/company/group may be working toward a similar goal. Can you help each other instead of competing for resources? Do your team goals support those of the organization?

The environment may reach beyond the workplace to the surrounding community. Sometimes, you must create a cohesive team to problem-solve with the larger community and critical stakeholders.

Are there individuals or organization representatives from other companies who should be apprised of your team's actions? When communicating with those outside of your immediate team, all critical communication rules apply. Keep the following in mind:

1. Listen.

3. Include representatives in the problem-solving process.

4. Acquire and share information.

5. Be consistent in your approach.

6. Acknowledge errors.

7. Acknowledge issues that are not easily resolved.

8. Be honest.

9. Keep channels of communication open.

10. Be accessible.

11. Be informed.

12. Be sincere.

Team Activity: Group Mandala

This exercise allows exploration of group structure and dynamics and reveals personal feelings towards others and one's own "place" in the structure. Logistically, a simple activity, although potentially difficult and challenging to facilitate, has lots of potential for subtle and deep group work. (Group sizes of approximately seven to nine are ideal, but it can be done with as few as five or as many as twelve.) This activity should take thirty to forty minutes.

What is a mandala? Mandalas are symbols of patterned interconnection within circles; mandala is Sanskrit for circle, polygon, community, and connection.

1. Each team member is asked to bring a personal object or an object from nature to represent themselves. (The object will be tossed and should not be too fragile.) This object, in the exercise, represents the person who brought it.

2. Team members form a circle and each person tosses his or her object into the center like dice.

3. Each person shares how he or she feels about the position in which his or her object has landed.

4. One by one, each person around the circle has the option to move his/her object to a new position, explaining to the group why it feels more comfortable for the object to be in this different place. This may take a few rounds.

5. Ask the group to discuss and collectively create (move/shift) objects into an ideal arrangement by consensus.

6. Debrief:
   • What did you learn?
   • How do you feel about your place in the team?
   • Did you learn anything about your feelings or notions about the team's dynamic that surprised you?
   • Did you learn anything about other team member's feelings or notions about the team's dynamic that surprised you?
   • What positive impressions did you have about the team prior to the activity that were reinforced?
   • What, if any, negative impressions were dispelled?

Facilitator Notes:

Participants could bring a surprising variety of objects; for example, an engagement ring, a pocket knife, a stone bearing the inscription "inspiration," a teddy bear, necklaces and rings, trinkets, and so on. Initially I did not ask participants to describe the significance of their objects—not asking this obvious question can heighten the sense of mystery and suspense in the activity. By the end of the activity, the participants responded favorably and more richly to an earlier hint that we might close the activity by sharing with others the personal significance associated with the object. This provided a deep, satisfying sense of closing to the activity.

Overall, the exercise works well, but it can be a challenge initially to process as there is often some resistance and anxiety associated with the apparent open-endedness of the activity.

—Adapted from "Group Mandala" by James Neill, researcher, lecturer, adventurer of the mind and planet, www.wilderdom.com

Means of Communication

We can send or receive information by information-sharing software, email, fax, instant message, voice mail, overnight carrier, or even old-fashioned snail mail. We can teleconference, virtual conference, or meet face-to-face (should we dare). The point is, we have choices. All choices do not apply in all situations. Choose your medium wisely to work most efficiently. Email and voice mail seem to create the most missed signals, but these can easily be avoided or reduced.

Email

For many, email is the easiest mode of communication, but is it always the best choice? No. Because email is such an efficient method of sending information, many people overuse and misuse it.

If your distribution list is overwhelming, know that much of what you send is going straight to the trash. In fact, it may end up in the trash by being automatically forwarded to a spam file or have been overlooked and accidentally deleted. When you call one team member to discuss a project, do you conference in four or five others? Why then must emails be copied to the world and beyond?

Email is also not as perfect as we would like it to be. If you find yourself saying, "I sent an email. What more should I do?" Stop and think about the answer. Look at the circumstances and the recipient. Consider choosing the phone or face-to-face over email or snail mail. What are the benefits? Do they save you time in the long run?

Consider your response to email. When you receive a letter in the mail, do you drop everything to respond immediately? Probably not. Your response time should be related to the importance and/or urgency of the message, not to the manner in which it is conveyed. For many, email creates a sense of urgency that rarely discriminates; just because emails come through almost instantaneously doesn't mean they have to be answered that very second.

Do not use email alone when:
- You need an immediate action or response, and you are not positive that the recipient is online. (Even if the recipient is online, that does not ensure that mail is being checked.)

- You need a discussion to resolve an issue.
- You need to express something diplomatically that will "play" better with the right tone of voice.
- You need to communicate something important and/or timely to someone who easily gets two hundred emails a day.

Voice Mail

"Phone tag" is a paralyzing waste of time that can cripple productivity and raise frustration levels. The more specific your message, the less need there is for a clarifying conversation about a simple request.

Message essentials:

Why are you calling?
- You need information, documents, other; be specific.
- You need the above by a certain date and time.
- You need to discuss a specific topic.

What response are you looking for?
- You would like the person or his/her designee to call you with information.
- You need to confirm a meeting, a plan, a cancellation.
- You need to speak directly with the person whom you are calling. If that person is not available, you need to know when you can connect. (Leave a time when you can be reached.)

What communication snags can you avoid?
- Never assume your number is on caller ID. If a cell phone is turned off or out of signal range, your number will not appear.
- Say your number twice for clarity; cell phones cut out.
- Most of us have multiple numbers; be clear about which is best to reach you on and when. If you ask people to get right back to you, don't have them try your office, both cell phones, and the home phone to find you; they probably won't bother.
- If you will be in meetings for the rest of the day, you need to make that clear, and confirm that leaving information on your voice mail will be fine.

Team Activity: Media Mania

Have team members work in small groups to identify a variety of media, when they use them, and the advantages and disadvantages (to both the sender and receiver) of the various media for different messages. Recommend that they think about specific times when a media choice worked well or caused a problem. Suggest that the team conclude this activity by creating media choice guidelines for increased productivity and decreased frustration.

Medium	Advantages	Disadvantages	When *Not* to Use

Chapter

Feedback

"If you have ideas and information that will help someone perform better, it's hostile not to share them." —Anne Saunier, consultant

- ▶ **Why Give Feedback?**
- ▶ **Positive Feedback**
- ▶ **Developmental Feedback**
- ▶ **Peer Feedback**
- ▶ **Assessing Team Leaders**
- ▶ **Client/Customer Feedback**
- ▶ **The Language of Feedback**
- ▶ **The Learning Process**

Why Give Feedback?

One of the most critical communication imperatives for growing businesses is feedback. Without it, team members risk working hard and doing an outstanding job at exactly the wrong thing. Feedback keeps team members and team leaders on track, clear about expectations, and confident in their contributions and abilities to support one another.

Develop Your Employees

Employee development through ongoing positive and developmental feedback, as well as job coaching, is one of the business owner's key responsibilities. Owners of growing companies often ask, "When do I have time?" Make time. Your business's success depends on it. Positive feedback keeps the good striving to do better and the better working to achieve their best. Developmental feedback is supportive and helps employees improve.

Team members want to know how they're doing. Share expectations and acknowledge that they have or have not been met. A lack of feedback creates the potential for several communication problems. It could lead to team members thinking they are meeting expectations when they are not, continually making the same mistakes, or believing their contributions are unnoticed, not valued, or unimportant.

Feedback Benefits

- Keeps team members on track
- Provides guidelines for improvement
- Contributes to increased productivity
- Increases morale
- Leads to greater job satisfaction
- Shows appreciation

The Feedback Loop

Feedback from the team leader or business owner to team members is only one of several feedback perspectives. The most effective feedback gives team members and team leaders input from the full circle of players including team leader, team members, clients, and customers, rounding it out with a self-assessment. In order to ensure that feedback is fair and the process is useful, establish a protocol.

Include all team members or representatives in creating a team feedback process. Instead of reinventing the wheel, your team may want to use or adapt one of many existing systems. Build in enough lead-time to announce the process so that everyone can understand the guidelines and participate without feeling pressured. Depending on how many employees you have, you may want to try a pilot program to get the kinks out before rolling out a large initiative.

Positive Feedback

Positive feedback is a means of acknowledging accomplishments and giving recognition. People who feel good about themselves produce positive results. In *The One Minute Manager*, Blanchard and Johnson coined the phrase "one-minute praisings." In today's fast-paced work environment, such moments are more important than ever. They regularly let people know that you value them and their contributions. Timely positive feedback is also important, so don't put the kudos on the back burner.

Often, caught in the press of getting things done, a business owner overlooks creating time—even a moment—to thank and to praise. Many tend to believe that those doing great jobs know it, so they choose to focus on bringing the slackers up to speed. Even your top performers need to know that they're appreciated.

How many times a day do you give positive feedback? Try using a simple system to help you answer that question and as a reminder to offer encouraging words throughout the day. Most importantly, your system should raise your awareness of building responsiveness to others into your day.

How to Do It

Positive feedback is too important to stress over doing it absolutely correctly. Just do it! Anything from a handwritten note or email (e.g., "Great job on XYZ!"), a public acknowledgement (formal or informal), approaching the employee informally with a compliment, or a phone call will do. The important thing is not to put it off until the moment is a distant memory.

"Quick hit" praise keeps people aware of your continuing appreciation of them and their work.

Often, an employee deserves more than the private pat on the back. If your junior account executive just received an outstanding commendation from a client, don't just zip over a "way to go" email; copy others in the chain of command or on the team. As the business owner, you can highlight team members' accomplishments in many ways. Following are just a few:

- Openly passing on the praise: "Thanks, but Henry is really the moving force behind that initiative."
- A kudos bulletin board in the coffee room, reception area, or an online bulletin board.
- Add a "pat on the back" moment to short morning or weekly meetings.
- Include a kudos corner in your company newsletter or online.

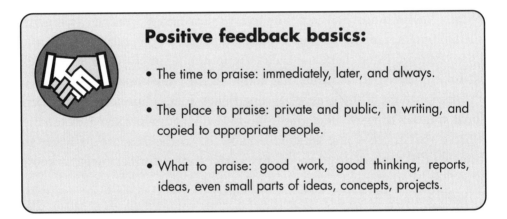

Positive feedback basics:

- The time to praise: immediately, later, and always.

- The place to praise: private and public, in writing, and copied to appropriate people.

- What to praise: good work, good thinking, reports, ideas, even small parts of ideas, concepts, projects.

Create a Positive Workplace

You want to create a culture in which everyone is a peak performer, earning praise periodically. An early mentor, Lee Digney used to say, "Behavior breeds behavior." Apply that principle. Some employees need a little more nurturing and support than others. The employer who looks at these employees as "drains" will surely reap that effect. The employer who finds the small thing to praise helps develop a lagging team member into a more confident and more productive one. Acknowledge small gains, and you will see larger ones.

Don't forget the particular value of feedback to those who work "behind the scenes" or in "the back of the house." They miss out on encouragement from interactions with clients and customers. Many don't even interact with colleagues or coworkers; yet their roles are vital to your company's success. Acknowledge them, and make a point of ensuring that others in you company know of and appreciate their contributions.

Finally, you might have a team that does everything required but lacks what it takes to push beyond. Positive feedback can ignite that spark. If you're from the "that's what a paycheck is for" school, you probably won't light any fires. Acknowledge the good job, praise the results, and provide encouragement. This sounds simple and straightforward. An unproductive approach would be to criticize, leading to a "What does he/she want from us?" reaction. Yes, running a business would be easier if everyone working in it were self-motivated. Some may be hesitant to go the extra mile for a myriad of reasons: baggage from previous negative work environments, fear of failure or of success; the list is endless. Your role is creating the workplace that motivates even those slow to light their own fires.

Developmental Feedback

Developmental feedback is both big picture and a critical detail. You want to encourage overall team and team member improvement and growth. You have to remain cognizant of slips, both small and large, that affect job performance and, consequently, customer satisfaction and your bottom line. Job coaching discussions may focus on overall lagging performance, specific behaviors, or issues that prevent employees from reaching their full potential and, consequently, negatively impact your output and the overall smooth functioning of a team.

Give developmental feedback when:
- A typically strong performer begins to slip
- A behavior affects the team's work product
- Unsettled issues or concerns persist
- Errors occur repeatedly
- Performance falls below average or changes drastically
- Follow-up is required on a particular issue or concern

How, When, and What to Discuss

The purpose of developmental feedback is to provide guidance and support, not to ridicule or demean. Productive developmental feedback is factual, specific, and behaviorally-based. Broad labels invariably produce defensiveness that derails useful discussion. Team members benefit most when they are presented with specific, concrete examples of behaviors or actions that require change or improvement. Ambiguous feedback or vague, general references may leave people confused and will not change future behavior.

Don't wait until you have a laundry list of problems before providing developmental feedback. Address concerns as they arise; don't wait until they may be more difficult to resolve or, even, beyond resolution. Effective feedback should be in digestible amounts and focused on identifying a limited number of significant behaviors. When too many behaviors are addressed at one time, the receiver may suffer from "feedback overload" and be unable or unwilling to change any behavior.

Discuss items that the employee can change. Useful feedback helps the receiver identify a performance problem and take corrective action. Most employees want to do well. When people are competent and confident, work is more rewarding. Often, people think they're doing the right thing and doing it well. Concrete developmental feedback not only helps the employees receiving it, but the team they are on and the company as a whole.

Follow up is as important as the feedback itself. Did the behavior change? Did the team member find the feedback helpful? Did he or she implement change? Schedule follow-up sessions to check in on progress. Monitor your own feedback style to determine whether your process is working. If you are unclear as to whether your feedback was helpful, ask. Make clear that you're interested in an honest evaluation of your feedback style. Be open to learning and growing through the process so that you can offer the best system of support and encouragement and be most effective in helping team members learn, grow, and excel in the future.

Fix the Problem: Stay focused on finding a solution rather than assigning blame by avoiding these pitfalls:

• Failing to reserve time for observation

• Falling into the black-and-white trap (everything is either urgent or not important)

• Succumbing to the halo (always right) or the muddy shoes (always wrong) effect

• Mistaking hearsay for the truth

• Presuming that good employees know they're good

• Failing to give frequent and timely feedback

• Talking too much; not listening

QUICK Tip

Developmental Feedback Must Be:

1. Specific

2. Factual

3. Behavior-based

4. Timely

5. Useful

6. Followed up

Seven-Step Developmental Feedback Model

1. **State the problem.**

   Begin the discussion by directly addressing the problem. Don't leave any doubt as to why you are meeting. Vague references or generalities will lead to an uncomfortable, unproductive discussion. Be clear about the behavior the employee must change, and use concrete examples. Start with, "You're always late," and you guarantee that the discussion will revolve around the times the employee hasn't been late. Instead try, "Maria, you arrived late today. This is the third time in two weeks you haven't been able to start your work until 8:15 a.m."

2. **State job-related consequences.**

   Show how the behavior is a problem that affects the employee's work as well as others'.

   "When you're not on time, others have to cover for you. You also miss the beginning of the a.m. team meetings, so you aren't up-to-date on issues that may affect the day's routine."

3. **Probe to identify the cause of the problem.**

   Ask questions, and wait for responses. Don't speculate or fill in the silence. By waiting, you require the other person to take responsibility and address the issue.

   "You have always been on time. What's the problem?"

4. **Listen actively.**

   Ensure that you understand the issue, and encourage the speaker to go on by repeating key phrases.

   "So, your day care center changed its hours and now opens at 7:30 a.m. Yes, this is difficult."

5. **Ask the team member for solutions.**

   Resist the urge to provide solutions. You are more likely to get employee "buy-in" for a solution that he or she generates, rather than one you provide.

   "What can you do to get to work on time even though the center opens later?"

6. **Develop a concise action plan with the team member.**

   Once the team member acknowledges the problem and searches for solutions, you can offer suggestions. Use questioning skills to ensure you are both on the same page. Gain commitment to the plan before moving forward.

"Yes, your day care carpooling idea would certainly cut down on the problem. Can you think of an additional solution? What about asking for your child to be accepted fifteen minutes early?"

7. **Summarize and set a time for follow-up.**

Once you've established an action plan, refrain from looking over the employee's shoulder. You both know what needs to be done—micromanaging will only lead to defensiveness.

"Let's talk this time next week to review how the changes you've decided to implement are working out."

Leadership Activity:
Following the Seven-Step Feedback Model

Following the feedback model is pretty straightforward. As with any skill, practice will strengthen your coaching technique. Use the example below or one of your own and role-play with a trusted colleague. If you have employees who coach others, engage them in a coaching practice session designed so that partners practice and an observer gives feedback, or partners practice and receive group feedback.

Coaching situation:

You recently instituted clear guidelines for Internet use. You have a small company that works on tight deadlines, and you require 100 percent accuracy in all correspondence that goes out through any vehicle. A new account executive, actually the employee who caused you—after so many years—to draft Internet use guidelines for your growing company, continues to instant message friends in the midst of writing documents. The distractions result in typos and evident inconsistencies. You have come to rely on all account executives being responsible for proofing and checking their own work.

Prepare for the feedback discussion: Write out your comments for steps 1 and 2 and the questions you would ask in step 3. Once you ask these questions, the conversation takes off as you follow the remaining steps.

Alert!

Feedback intention check: Check your intentions. Is your feedback appropriate? Is it intended to help or praise? Does your feedback on a particular situation have more to do with your own ego or being "right"? Think it through first. If you find your own ego lurking behind the feedback, put it to the side, and consider whether the feedback is truly valid and necessary. If not, drop it. If so, realize you need to be especially careful in choosing your words and tone.

QUICK Tip

Correcting behavior: No one on your team should be treated badly. If one team member is disrespectful or abusive (shouting, put downs, etc.), then you have a responsibility to take that person aside and be clear that such behavior has no place on your team. A word of caution: go easy. Sometimes these people aren't quite as tough as they seem and may not realize how their behavior is affecting others. "How can that be?" you and everyone around them might wonder.

Don't start by assuming they know what they're doing. In these busy, fast-paced times, what people don't know about themselves may astound you. We tend to judge books by their covers and people by their outward personas, the images that they show us. We also expect people to see and hear themselves, which is not always the case. A little developmental feedback could be all they need to listen to themselves and adjust their behavior, making them more pleasant and productive coworkers and employees.

Peer Feedback

Peer feedback is an opportunity for coworkers to reinforce one another's positive roles, behaviors, and contributions, and to gain insight into performance issues that affect the team's progress or work environment. Colleagues should be encouraged to express their views, discuss how each teammate is aiding/reinforcing the others, or suggest ways to improve a less-than-ideal or difficult situation. Team feedback may be written, then reviewed privately, or given within a structured feedback meeting.

Set Some Ground Rules

Team feedback requires proper, agreed-upon channels and a team that is informed about the benefits of using concrete language and providing feedback as a way to strengthen the team. Team balance dictates that any developmental feedback follow clear guidelines to ensure the most receptivity. Within such a framework, team members can provide suggestions and strategies for improving performance. Teams should be encouraged to share informal feedback, as well. These dialogues serve as excellent teambuilding tools.

Either way, team feedback in a supportive environment has impact. Think of training programs you may have attended or conducted. Whether giving a presentation or participating in a role-playing activity, direct, peer feedback creates change and facilitates learning. The same is applicable to the team meeting after a product launch, a client meeting, or a "stormy day at the office." Peer feedback opens minds, offers insights, and creates additional bonds.

Start with Questions

The typical training model begins with, "How do you think you did? What about your presentation do you think went well? What would you change?" or "Do you believe that you were effective in the role? What did you say that was particularly effective? What didn't work well?"

Apply that model to your team meeting. Who needs the feedback? How would you frame the questions? Try to develop standard questions for specific debrief meetings so everyone feels comfortable and fairly treated.

Developmental feedback from one team member to another is an especially delicate issue. Team members cannot be made to feel that they are suddenly "working for" colleagues. Whether from a team member or team leader, feedback should be focused, private (unless a public team feedback session is established), and based strictly on work-related behavior with clearly stated work-related consequences. If corrective action is necessary, a team leader should jointly determine that action with the team member. If, however, the feedback comes from another team member or the team as a whole, corrective action may be inappropriate. No team member should overstep bounds or claim seniority unless it has been predetermined by the group.

Positive feedback from team members is core to individual motivation and, consequently, the team as a whole. The team should follow team feedback guidelines when raising concerns and praising. Distribute or post the Team Feedback Guidelines.

Figure 5.1: TEAM FEEDBACK GUIDELINES

Feedback should be:

1. Specific.
2. Based on facts and/or observable behavior.
3. Focused on behavior that the recipient has the power to change.
4. Intended to develop, support, or praise rather than punish or embarrass.
5. Descriptive rather than judgmental.
6. Given in an appropriate setting.
7. Timely.

QUICK Tip

Nipping trouble in the bud: Garvey Shubert & Barer, a Seattle, Washington–based law firm, established a Collegiality Committee to intercept counterproductive behavior at the earliest opportunity. This committee meets with the employee responsible for the offensive comment or behavior, states the problem, and explores with the offender avenues for resolution and change.

Team Activity: Building Egos for Team Strength

Often, during the press of the workday, we think positive thoughts about those on our team but don't make the time to verbalize them. Additionally, we may have strained our less than smooth relationships with others on our team, creating a blind spot to those things they do well. This activity is designed to, as the old song says, "accentuate the positive."

Directions:

1. Write each team member's name on a piece of paper or print out a list and cut it into strips. Fold each name and put it into a basket.

2. Pass the collection around until each person pulls a name (other than his/her own).

3. For one minute, have each person list, in writing, as many positive attributes as possible for the team member drawn (e.g., helpful, open, a good listener).

4. For one minute, have each person write a behavioral example for each characteristic listed (e.g., helpful—always pitches in, never turns down a request for assistance; open—shares information and ideas freely).

5. As a group, have each person, in turn, identify the team member described and verbally give that person the positive feedback just generated. As each team member completes his/her feedback, ask if anyone in the group has anything to add.

6. Before moving on to the next team member, ask each person receiving the feedback the following questions:

   • Is that how you view yourself? Please explain.

   • Did you realize that team members viewed you this way?

   • Any comments?

7. Ask team members to hand the written notes to the members to whom they apply. Unfortunately, we often have a short memory for such things, and it helps to come away with the written praise.

8. Generate a discussion about the exercise and how it might positively impact the team. Ask for suggestions for maintaining the positive environment created.

Team Activity: Learning Curve

Start by having each team member consider a circumstance that did not go well—either one they believe they could have handled differently or one they think was completely out of their control.

Team member self-assessment questions:

1. My most recent crisis:

2. My post-assessment of my reaction/response/resolution:

3. What would I do differently?

Team input:

Each team member then shares the situation. The group's task is to come up with three—no more, no less—possible improvements to handling an issue. This way, team members can see that even a situation that was handled well might be handled better the next time and have the benefit of useful feedback from the group. Limit to three suggestions so that the person who has made mistakes is not bombarded or made to feel as though everyone in the room would have handled the problem better. Emphasize, too, that this exercise is easy for team members sitting in a room after the fact. Stress that everyone appreciates the difficulties faced with being "in the moment" of a crisis.

Encourage team members to also offer praise and positive reinforcement for areas they believe were handled well and to openly express how hearing another team member's particular crisis and resolution (individual and team) was personally helpful. Remind everyone of the Monday morning quarterback's "perfect" calls (filling in the blanks for anyone who might miss the reference).

Assessing Team Leaders

Receiving feedback is as important as providing it; be prepared to receive as well as give. Your openness to feedback strengthens not only your performance, but your team's. It creates an atmosphere respectful of ongoing dialogue and, consequently, opportunities for business improvement.

Receiving Feedback

Being receptive to feedback starts with setting feedback expectations and creating a climate of sharing rather than one of fear. Team members may be afraid of repercussions in offering feedback to their superior; your job is to make this as comfortable as possible. Invite ongoing feedback through feedback forums, meetings, one-to-one interactions, or in writing. Hearing team member feedback can offer you personal growth as well as a chance to meet team needs, which might have otherwise gone unexpressed.

As appropriate, modify your behavior in suggested directions and then evaluate the outcomes. Employees or team members who give feedback to those in leadership positions are positively affected by knowing that their voices were heard.

A by-product of receiving feedback from your team is that you see firsthand how each expresses his/her feelings about others' work. Do not respond to your feedback with a lesson on how to give feedback. Store that information to address at a more appropriate time and without referencing your experience. When you are the recipient of feedback, your role is to process what you are hearing and to show that you care about team member concerns. Remember that even if the delivery could be more eloquent and sensitive, it is up to you to focus on content.

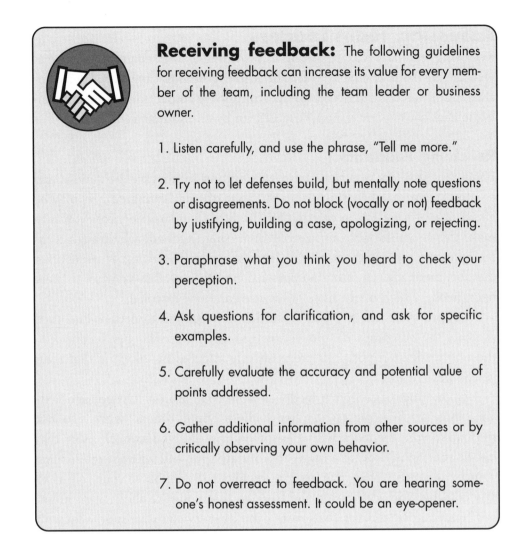

Receiving feedback: The following guidelines for receiving feedback can increase its value for every member of the team, including the team leader or business owner.

1. Listen carefully, and use the phrase, "Tell me more."

2. Try not to let defenses build, but mentally note questions or disagreements. Do not block (vocally or not) feedback by justifying, building a case, apologizing, or rejecting.

3. Paraphrase what you think you heard to check your perception.

4. Ask questions for clarification, and ask for specific examples.

5. Carefully evaluate the accuracy and potential value of points addressed.

6. Gather additional information from other sources or by critically observing your own behavior.

7. Do not overreact to feedback. You are hearing someone's honest assessment. It could be an eye-opener.

Client/Customer Feedback

Include your clients or customers in the feedback process. Only by discovering what your customers need and value can you tailor your products and services to them and exceed their expectations. Identifying criteria used by your customers to choose, assess, or continue to use your products or services will strengthen marketing and sales initiatives.

The best way to know what your clients and customers want is to ask and to listen. Customer feedback is essential to business success. Unfortunately, it is not easy to elicit unless you've upset or disappointed them. Those customers do exist who go out of their way to offer positive feedback or praise a specific team member. They are not, however, in the majority.

How often have you left a hotel or restaurant intending to complete the feedback form but never getting around to it? Have you ever gotten the follow-up survey link in your email and saved it until it was so long ago it didn't seem relevant anymore? Most people, even those with the best intentions and highest praise, get busy. What's the answer? You will never receive a 100 percent feedback rate, so put some emphasis on eliciting responses. As a growing business, organize your feedback process to include representative customers in your initial process notification and guidelines. Emphasize the importance of the customer component.

Figure 5.2: **SEVEN WAYS TO INCREASE CUSTOMER FEEDBACK**

1. Provide an easy response form; don't count on people going out of their way without an easy-return form of some kind.

2. Make your form as simple and brief as possible to increase the odds of someone filling it in on the spot. Forms left for later are, most often, tossed.

3. Provide more than one method for response; an email or drop-in-a-box response card can also include your Web address with a simple, easy-to-find online form.

4. Develop a brief three-to-five-question telephone survey of your most pertinent questions. As always, the last question should be for additional comments.

5. For product orders, enclose a three-to-five-question survey on a postcard with your order. Always ask for additional comments.

6. Send an email requesting a one-sentence quote to use with your promotional literature.

7. If you use more than one method for feedback, keep records. Repeated calls and email requests to someone who has already filled out your survey online may elicit a new, less gratified survey response and could cause you to lose a valuable customer.

Getting Deeper

For more in-depth feedback, schedule annual, semiannual, or quarterly (depending upon your business and your client/customer base) meetings to discuss your client's/customer's changing needs and ways you might address them. Integrate feedback questions into the discussion. You'll learn about what you've been doing right, what you could do better, and what you have to change to continue to meet each client's needs. These might be face-to-face, by telephone, or web conferencing.

Your clients/customers may express a need that you cannot stretch to meet. Be honest and, if possible, refer a qualified source. Follow up with both the referred provider and the customer/client. You want to know what went right—or wrong.

The Language of Feedback

Words and phrases can carry different meanings for different people. Many are wide open to subjective interpretation either based on tone or on meanings that are less than precise. What does "rarely" mean to you? Every few years? A few times a year? Every other month? Of course, that's a hard question to answer because, for all of us, it changes with context. If I say Jim rarely initiates ideas in our daily meetings, that could mean anything from once every two weeks to once or twice per year.

When using subjective words, use examples and time frames whenever possible; be sure that your meaning is clear to the feedback recipient. Talk about specifics: "The past two times that we met..."; "Each month when our team report is due..."; "This is the third time that...." Otherwise, your comments could have no impact other than creating defensiveness or confusion. Be careful when using words on the following list, especially "never" and "always," which, in giving developmental feedback, are never quite accurate and always inflammatory.

- ALWAYS
- Often
- Frequently
- Usually
- Periodically
- Regularly

- Habitually
- Perpetually
- Sometimes
- On occasion
- Now and then
- Seldom
- Rarely
- Hardly ever
- NEVER

Words should describe, not evaluate. How helpful are these statements?
- "You obviously don't want to contribute to this report."
- "Your attitude needs improvement."
- "Your workflow is below average."
- "People say you're very argumentative."
- "You have a bad attitude. Shape up."
- "You need to be a better team player."
- "Get on the ball."

Even positive feedback is more useful and/or inspiring when concrete language is used. How inspiring is the generic comment?
- "You do good work."
- "Fine job."
- "We couldn't get along without you."
- "Glad you're on our team."
- "People tell me you're a good team player."

Leadership Activity: Watch Your Language!

Think about an instance in which you would use each of the following words. Name the specific behavior(s) or action(s) that would illustrate each evaluative word or phrase. For example, a person who is "disruptive" may regularly interrupt colleagues during meetings, when they are on the phone, or focusing on a client or customer.

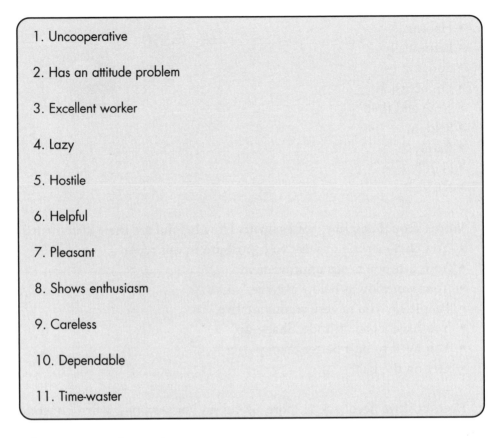

1. Uncooperative

2. Has an attitude problem

3. Excellent worker

4. Lazy

5. Hostile

6. Helpful

7. Pleasant

8. Shows enthusiasm

9. Careless

10. Dependable

11. Time-waster

The Learning Process

We're all learning every day. We make mistakes and hopefully, through self, peer, and team leader guidance, we learn to make improvements and adjustments to ensure smoother operation the next time. Remember the often-repeated maxim that if you're not making mistakes you're not learning.

Be patient during team development—remember your own trials and learning processes as you tested new waters—to better understand and troubleshoot as your team members learn. Helpful, constructive, and supportive team members can be crucial in each other's professional growth and development.

As you develop your team with training, new initiatives, and new processes, encourage questions. Simulate as much as you can in the learning environment so that mistakes will more likely be made there than on the job. Encourage participants to overcome any shyness within the learning environment where mistakes should be treated as welcome learning opportunities.

QUICK Tip

Practice makes perfect: I think it's important to create a supportive learning environment where people are comfortable knowing that if they don't do well no one's judging them. They're just there to practice until the moment that they have to perform. I tell my class that the more you participate and the more you practice the better you'll get at selling. Presentations need to be practiced out loud. You just can't look at it and say, "Okay, I think I got it," and then walk into a room under very stressful conditions and sell. But if you just practice—even if you read it and fumble and everything's wrong—you'll be much more prepared.

I always use a golf analogy to put practice into perspective. We're on the driving (or practice) range where people hit buckets and buckets of balls. They hit hundreds and thousands of golf balls looking only for a few really great shots, but more looking to find their rhythm and swing. The best way to emulate this determination to improve is in class with five or six people at a table practicing skills with your peers, letting them evaluate you, and getting feedback from them. You don't want to just watch other people because you don't get better watching; you get better by practicing and learning from your mistakes. So, basically, we're all on the driving range every day.

The more I say, over time, "We're all on the driving range," the more people buy in and soon, if someone doesn't do well, they're all saying, "Hey, it's okay. It's just the practice range. We're not on the golf course yet." When people begin to assimilate that idea, their practice becomes more relaxed and more valuable.

—Matthew Odette, sales trainer

Team Activities: Sports

Team sports are classic team builders. The company softball team is a standard but doesn't include everyone or make everyone feel like part of the team. Where success is more important than inclusion, the essence of teambuilding is lost.

Pick a sport that allows you to improvise games to include people of different skill levels. Always create team mixes that put those who rarely or never played the sport with those who are highly proficient. People with different proficiencies and skill levels working together to achieve a goal is the basic definition of any team. Sports are also a great way for team members to practice patient instruction, constructive feedback, and positive reinforcement.

Golf: Pick a small course that is friendly to nongolfers, and have participants play out nine holes. Each team member takes a turn, counting the number of strokes each team takes to sink the ball. Divide teams as fairly as you can. Set a maximum number of strokes per hole so that a team is allowed to move on and not be stuck indefinitely at a difficult hole. If golfers on your team have other notions of how to devise a simple game that involves everyone, allow them to be creative and run the exercise.

Bowling: Bowling lends itself to a fun team outing. To level the playing field, play a regular game and then switch to using nondominant hands.

Fun Prizes: To include everyone in the fun, offer small prizes (team and individual), not only for scores, but for most improved. Get input from the team, before the game, on some of the special prizes to be awarded. Allow anything, as long as it's not offensive to anyone.

Chapter  6

The Culture Mix

"For those who have seen the Earth from space, and for the hundreds and perhaps thousands more who will, the experience most certainly changes your perspective. The things that we share in our world are far more valuable than those which divide us." —Donald Williams, Astronaut

- ▶ Culture Consciousness
- ▶ Language and the Multicultural Team
- ▶ Traveling Abroad
- ▶ Generational "Cultures"
- ▶ Culture Chasms

Culture Consciousness

Our work environments are more of a cultural, social mix than ever before, with a wider age range running through them as young talents skip or sail through "entry level" and those who, in another era, would have been "retirement ready" remain active members of the workforce (by choice or necessity). By doing our best to understand both the differences and similarities among multiple age groups and cultures, we can improve our communication within our companies and teams. This culturally diverse work arena, the multinational company, the multicultural customer and client base, as well as the attendant virtual element bringing global organizations together like never before, create the need for heightened culture consciousness.

Tools for Cultural Consciousness

Awareness and respect are essential when working with anyone with a different background or perspective from yours. Awareness tunes you in to why others may behave or react differently from your concept of "the norm." Respect ensures that whether or not you accept or even understand the difference, you are respectful of the other person. Though we cannot understand every culture we might encounter, we can understand that cultural differences exist and give the benefit of the doubt when behavior seems awkward by our standards. By knowing that, for example, North Americans view direct eye contact as a sign of honesty, those unfamiliar with that custom should not be offended by it. On the flip side, knowing that Asians view direct eye contact as a form of disrespect, Americans should not misjudge a lowering of the eyes.

The extra mile on both sides is changing behavior somewhat to make the other more comfortable. In some businesses, it's more than the extra mile; it's a necessity. If a company's customer-friendly policy requires a warm smile and handshake, cultural backgrounds aside, comfort levels must be stretched, but the request should be made with sensitivity to the difficulty of "unlearning" cultural customs.

One common cause for discomfort is the variety of personal space protocols and comfort zones. North Americans are known for closing the space gap, stepping in with the handshake. Some cultures want to really get close and make even some North Americans uncomfortable, while others choose to shake hands at a two arms' length distance.

Cultural differences go well beyond eye contact and body language. Some cultures use, respect, and expect precise language: "around 30 percent" isn't enough information. They want to hear "31.5 percent." Others may not want to disappoint by saying, "No," so they throw your entire schedule off by waffling and leading you to believe that they will attend the inconveniently scheduled meeting. Also, negotiation styles, comfort levels with talking about personal issues, when and how to ask about financial specifics, and minute details you might never think of can affect how smooth your multicultural interactions are.

Differences you might encounter:

• **Time:** Does 10:00 a.m. mean 10:00 a.m. or 10:10 or 10:30? Just as you may perceive the late arrival as rude, those from cultures embedded with "don't arrive on time," may find the punctual—or worse yet, early—arrival rude, not to mention inconvenient.

• **Tradition:** Open the gift now in front of everyone, or take it home to open privately?

• **Trust:** For those from cultures that customarily conduct business with a handshake, insistence on the written agreement may seem insulting. Explanation and understanding are crucial.

• **Regulations:** Even within the same company, a team member in one country may want to move an approval process quickly while his/her counterpart across the Atlantic won't budge without working through a cumbersome trail of required signatures.

• **Dietary restrictions:** Planning a company event for a mixed cultural team? Keep in mind that some won't eat dairy, some won't eat meat (or certain meats). And those might be all Americans! Don't go crazy, but have a reasonable mix.

Cross-cultural customer care: Nowhere is awareness more critical to your business success than in your relationships with your customers. They have no stake in understanding you. You have every reason to choose to understand them. If your company is serving a multicultural customer base either in the U.S. or abroad, don't "guess" about language, customs, or protocols. If no one on your internal team has the relevant cultural experience, hire an external expert to guide you or at least give you a foundation of understanding basic differences.

QUICK Tip

Learning vs. judgment: Anthropologists discovered that, when faced by interaction that we do not understand, people tend to interpret the others involved as "abnormal," "weird," or "wrong." Awareness of cultural differences and recognizing where cultural differences are at work is the first step toward understanding each other and establishing a positive working environment. Use these differences to challenge your own assumptions about the "right" way of doing things and as a chance to learn new ways to solve problems.

—Vadim Kotelnikov, author and founder of Ten3 Business e-Coach, www.1000ventures.com

QUICK Tip

"Many nonnative English speakers need time to process what has been said and pick up on the nuances of American accents. Keep in mind that some people from other cultures may have a short processing delay for translation time. Be aware of pace in meetings and team process sessions to keep everyone in the loop."

—Natalie Gast, principal, Customized Language Skills Training, Little Falls, NJ, www.language-specialists.com

Language and the Multicultural Team

Americans are so immersed in the American idiom and slang that we often don't realize what an idiom is or how strange a direct translation might sound to a nonnative speaker of English who isn't familiar with many of our expressions.

When working with people from other cultures, be aware that expressions don't always translate easily, and, while some can be figured out, many like "in the black," "in the bag," "out of the blue," and "skin of your teeth" are meaningless to those who aren't in our cultural "know." We stick our necks out, bite bullets, take curves, often with hands tied or two left feet. What does any of that mean in direct translation? Direct translations often don't work, even if we're not using idioms, so think of how complicated translations become when we do.

Translators: An Intercultural Team Element

The human touch is essential for capturing the subtleties of translation; do not rely exclusively on computer-generated translations. Use a professional translator who has knowledge not only of the language you want to use, but of the culture: expressions, customs, and taboos. If the translator is unfamiliar with your industry, specialized content, or "jargon," you will need someone from your company to work closely throughout the process. Language among speakers of English is tricky enough. Putting your words in print in another language is a step that requires a professional company and strong vigilance.

If you work closely with people from various countries, you may each have some knowledge of the other's language; however, translation gaffes do occur. Treat them as learning experiences if you're the one making the mistakes. Treat them lightly and supportively when made by others. Tread gently, however. Humor doesn't always translate well.

QUICK Tip

Team up for translation: Teamwork is our whole life here. A project manager looks over the client's English document and clarifies ambiguities before the translation team begins. The translator and editor correspond all during the project to choose just the right wording for a phrase. The proofreading gives a translation the final polish. But where we really function as a team is helping the client identify inappropriate images, suggesting layouts that will handle the expansion of translated text, or working with their design team to create web-enables or print-ready PDFs so nothing is lost between our office and theirs.

—Patricia May, president and CEO, Precision Language Services, Lakeville, MN, www.precisionlanguage.com

Translation Troubles

Have you ever wondered what kind of reaction you would get if you tried to blow away your clients or team members with your sudden fluency in their languages by using a free online translator? Worse yet, did you ever try to translate copy for print or online? Free online translators are great for picking up a word or simple phrase here and there or getting a general meaning for yourself, but don't count on a computerized translator for language that you will put out in advertising, letters and emails, or any written communication or representation of your company. Often, grammar and word order are lost and sometimes sense is, too.

Here's a simple phrase translated to French then back into English: "I am afraid of muddled translations hurting my reputation," becomes: "I am afraid of has mixed-up of the translations injuring my reputation." Now, let's toss in an idiomatic expression. Here are translations (again, translated back to English) of the phrase: "I hope to blow my clients away with my sudden language fluency. Free translators are great!"

- **Russian:** "I hope to blow off my clients with my sudden fluency of language. Free translators are big!"
- **Spanish:** "I expect to blow my clients far away with my sudden fluency of language. The translators free they are great!"

- **French:** "I hope to crush my customers with my language ease sudden. The free translators are big!"
- **German:** "I hope to blow my customers away with my sudden language frequency. Translator pleased are large!"
- **Portuguese:** "I am going to drag my clients with my sudden fluency of language. Free translators are big!"
- **Dutch:** "I hope to blow my customers way with my sudden language vloeiendheid. Going out translators are tremendous!"

There is no substitute for a professional. Or as the Dutch would seem to say: "There is no vervangmiddel for a specialist."

Figure 6.1: LEGENDARY GLOBAL "OOPSES"

- Pepsi, using the slogan "Come alive with the Pepsi Generation" in China where the translation claimed: "Pepsi brings your ancestors back from the grave."

- Colgate's marketing of a toothpaste called Cue in France, not realizing that Cue is the name of a notorious French porno magazine.

- Clairol's "Mist Stick" curling iron introduced in Germany, where "mist" is slang for manure.

- Frank Perdue unwittingly proclaiming: "It takes an aroused man to make a chicken affectionate" in the Spanish translation of his slogan, "It takes a strong man to make a tender chicken."

- Electrolux (Scandinavian vacuum manufacturer) campaign in the U.S.: "Nothing sucks like an Electrolux." (Catchy, isn't it?)

- An American T-shirt maker printing shirts to promote the Pope's visit that said "I saw the potato" (la papa) instead of "I saw the Pope" (el Papa).

QUICK Tip

"Human diversity makes tolerance more than a virtue; it makes it a requirement for survival."

—Rene Dubos, *Celebrations of Life*, 1981

Alert!

Watch your phrasing and gestures: In Britain, to "table" something means to bring it to the table for discussion. In the U.S. it means to put it aside. I was in a meeting when an American suggested tabling a topic—and a British colleague opened a whole discussion around it. The outcome wasn't as planned. The American got annoyed with what he saw as English arrogance by someone who deliberately did it to make him angry, while the Englishman was bemused at the lack of interest and hostility around the table.

—Val Boyko, My Global Coach, Philadelphia, PA, myglobalcoach.com

Language differences also extend to gestures. What we know as the symbol for "OK" (sometimes zero) in the U.S. and UK is the symbol for zero in Russia, money in Japan, and is an insult in Brazil.

Sports Terms and Analogies in a Shrinking World

Beyond the idioms is a more easily recognized culture and language chasm: sports terms and analogies. Sports terms are an integral part of North American business language. We talk about stepping up to the plate, hitting a home run, or striking out, and no one likes to be thrown a curve ball. But is it possible that in this incredibly shrinking world that sports language as an integral part of business culture may be off base? You may want team players to toe the line, but what does that mean to someone who doesn't know what toeing the line means?

While sports terms are useful for those who can relate to them, they mean nothing to someone from a country that doesn't have those expressions, much less the sports from which they derived. Even the best players won't be inspired by terms they cannot relate to or fully understand. So your inspiring baseball stories and your "MVP" pats on the back may be having an opposite, divisive effect if you make someone feel like an outsider.

Even those immersed in the culture who simply aren't interested in sports will be left out, men and women alike. While many women are sports fans, others have had to learn sports terms just to keep up to speed in the boardroom. As women became a stronger force in the workplace, the sports jargon didn't adapt; sporting business-minded women did, and books like *Hardball for Women* came out to help us understand the language, game plans, and plays of a sports-oriented business culture. Now, with the global expansion factor present in so many businesses (especially in this Internet age), this hardball sports culture may have to watch its language and be more cognizant of using analogies and terms that everyone can understand.

How many executives does it take to lift a bench? Several executives were talking about changing the way they hire, adding more "bench strength," (referring to the strength of the lineup of players on the bench). The women in the boardroom, not a baseball fan among them, looked to one another for clues. After the meeting, they pooled their best guesses (bench pressing? bench lifting?) and "figured out" that it had to do with bench presses. While they got the gist— strong team—and were lucky enough to have each other, the baseball reference can leave a lot of intelligent people out in left field.

Traveling Abroad

When doing business abroad, learn as much as you can about the country's culture (overall and business) before you go. Consume books, surf the Net, talk to people who have had experiences with that culture. A few sessions with a cross-cultural business consultant can also be a tremendous help in getting you up to speed.

When packing clothes or thinking protocol, trust the experts over your gut feelings. Go ready to learn and ready to adapt. Forget flaunting your style; remember—"When in Rome…"

But the Book Said...

Imagine you're a woman business owner traveling to another country. You've read books or taken a quick-hit seminar on the culture. You know how to dress, how to behave, even appropriate table manners. You are visiting a very conservative culture. Then, your thirty-something, female business counterpart turns all the rules upside down: meets you in a skirt that grazes her knees, extends her hand, makes jokes, and creates a generally comfortable, casual atmosphere. She had been educated in the United States and readily puts you at ease. Her business associates are all around the same age and have been similarly educated, either in the U.S. or England.

So, you decide that nothing you've heard about this country and its customs is true, at least not anymore. What was that consultant thinking? Clearly, this is a new generation. In preparation for your next encounter at another client company the following morning, you use those rusty sewing skills and shorten that skirt that you knew was too long. You now feel at home. No longer concerned about the cultural faux pas, you've stopped focusing on what you've learned. You bound into your next meeting in your newly-shortened skirt, hand extended, large grin, and ready "funny" icebreaker. The sixty-something gentleman who greets you is not amused, but immediately aloof and on guard.

Just as differences abound in the U.S., so they do abroad. And nowhere are they more apparent than among different generations. Your safest route is a cautious one: watch, listen, and take cues. Don't assume "they're all alike." No two people are. But learn the "rules" of a country, and, when in doubt, err on the conservative side.

Figure 6.2: TWELVE TIPS FOR GLOBAL BUSINESS TRAVELERS

1. Learn something about the country, local customs, and cultural sensitivities to avoid making faux pas while abroad.

2. Err on the side of formality. Be low-key in dress, manners, and behavior.

3. Don't rush greetings and introductions in an effort to get down to business quickly.

4. Expect your meetings and negotiations to be longer than anticipated. Build more time into schedules.

5. Don't show impatience or irritation. Politeness and respect matter.

6. Express yourself carefully. Accents, idioms, and business jargon may be unfamiliar.

7. Listen attentively to show that you care about what is being said.

8. Indicate a sincere interest in your colleagues, their concerns and issues, to build win-win solutions.

9. Don't put global colleagues on the spot or cause loss of face by being too direct or expecting a "yes" or "no" answer.

10. Avoid public criticism or comparison with your own country.

11. Familiarize yourself with customs surrounding gift-giving and business entertaining.

12. Build relationships and trust, which is the key to successful global part-nerships.

—Contributed by Sondra Sen, Sheri Sen International, Inc., Mountain Lakes, NJ, www.sherisentsi.com

Generational "Cultures"

Beyond the confusion of integrating generational styles into our cross-cultural understanding, we have differences within our own country created by generations that are each, in some way, their own subcultures. Each generation has been shaped by events and values unique to it. Understanding the drivers and cautions of other generations helps all work better as teammates.

In a fast-paced, highly technological and increasingly virtual business culture in which college graduates (and dropouts, too) are CEOs, our young workforce often tends to overlook the value of their senior colleagues' perspectives. Many senior colleagues lament what they see as the end of the "work ethic" in the younger generation when they see less structure regarding hours, dress, and virtual commuting. While the work ethic has not ended, it is different, in large part, because of a dramatically changed work environment. Misinterpretations cause tension and deprive us of opportunities to build on each other's strengths.

There are so many generations in the workplace today that trying to understand your colleagues, supervisors, and employees can seem overwhelming. Once you've figured it all out, you realize that no one is a walking generalization: we are individuals.

As groups within our own generations, however, we do have shared memories, and that leads to some commonly-held mindsets and expectations. It is up to each one of us to overcome the limitations of these and let go of judgments or restrictions they impose on other generations. In true teamwork form, we can also nudge our generational peers when we see them getting stuck in a thought groove that has more to do with our own "times" than with a broader, more inclusive sensibility. Just the same, we can ask for that "nudge" in return. We are all products, to some degree, of our times. We have been so immersed in the world as we have experienced it that, like anyone immersed, we can easily lose a sense of perspective.

Figure 6.3: FREEZE AND REFRAME

When you say...	Ask yourself...
We tried that ten years ago; it didn't work. **or** I know what works; I've tried it all.	Everything has changed. Could an approach that didn't work then have simply been before its time?
Doesn't anybody listen?	Am *I* listening?
No one respects experience.	Do *I* respect new ideas?
No one wants to hear new ideas.	Do *I* respect others' experience? How am I presenting my ideas?
This is the way we have always done things.	Is there an even better way?
There is no history or continuity in this organization (department) anymore.	Am I afraid of change?
He or she could have saved days of research just by asking me a few questions.	Have I made myself open to questions? Did he or she learn anything new that I might learn from?
I don't get respect!	Do *I* respect others?
Who cares? Whatever!	Is it really hopeless enough to give up caring? How can I make this situation better?

Team Activity: What Are Your Expectations?

We discussed awareness as an important concept in understanding and accepting others. Have team members work in small groups to complete this exercise. A sample answer follows the activity box in case your team needs additional direction.

Step 1: Judgment Column—Write down your criticism/judgment.

Step 2: Behaviors Column—What is a specific behavior that is identifiable and not personal?

Step 3: Reality Checklist Column—For each behavior, return to this list, and ask the following four questions:

1. Is my expectation or judgment based on my experience in the past?

2. Is that still valid?

3. Did I examine actions and requests on their own merit, not on comparisons?

4. Is my expectation reasonable and fair?

Judgments	Behaviors	Reality Checklist

Sample Answer:

Judgments	Behaviors	Reality Checklist
Younger employees don't understand they have to pay their dues.	Kerri asked for an expense account; I didn't get one for two years.	While an expense account may have once meant status, times have changed. There is room in the budget. It will help Kerri entertain clients. It will cut down on bookkeeping.

Language Gaps

Generations not only have their own cultures, they have their own languages. Generational expressions are born of shared memories, references, and shorthand terms. Many out of a generation's loop may easily feel their younger or older coworkers have slipped into speaking another language entirely. Younger coworkers may feel that you are talking down to them if you aren't careful, and older coworkers can feel intentionally shut out. Be aware of the language you use. What is jargon?

You come back from an event and say it was like a mosh pit in there. You make a reference to Haight Ashberry. You toss out a reference to Duke Ellington. How many people in the room will look at you with blank stares? How many will ask? How many will just feel that you're out of the loop or that they are? Do you do this often in cross-generational or cross-cultural settings? Doing so can deepen your sense of "being alone out there" or make you appear to be insensitive to others, simply amusing yourself with very private jokes.

Of course, if you were to give background in making the comparison or comment, you would be bonding more than separating, creating a deeper understanding through sharing. Surely, those who don't know that a mosh pit is the area in front of the stage where audience members "mosh" or that Haight Ashberry was a famous 1960s hippie hangout in San Francisco that became a cultural icon could find it all very interesting and enjoy your clever comparison and appreciate being "let in." The only caution here is not to sound condescending, assuming others don't know anything about your culture or times.

Culture Chasms

Think about your relationships with those in your family, your neighborhood, your peer group, your friends. These are all people with whom you have some commonality. Some relationships you've chosen; some you haven't. But common threads tie you together. Yet—oh, the differences. You have disagreements and misunderstandings. You sometimes wonder, "How can we possibly be siblings?" "Why doesn't this friend understand my perspective?" "Are we really from the same planet?" These are thoughts you have about the people you know and love best; it can be even worse with a coworker.

Then we enter the workplace, physical or virtual, and expect people from different eras, cultures, regions, or countries to think, process, and act as we do. Reality is, however, that our cultures define much of who we are, our values and norms, and how we process, function, and interact. Cultural differences run the gamut from global cultures to regional, generational, and even subcultures within these. Even our own families are cultures unto themselves where we may have learned slightly different social norms or practiced different family customs from our neighbors. Being aware of our cross-cultural similarities—and we all have them—bridges the gap in some way, but so does being aware and respectful of differences.

Team Activity: What Do You Know about Yourself and Others on Your Team?

Have team members work with partners to answer the following questions. Ideally, partners should represent different cultural and/or age groups. Once each member of each partnership has a chance to answer the questions, discuss answers as a group. Ask what team members learned about themselves and others. Ask how these lessons can strengthen the team. Then, look at how the lessons learned can enhance customer/client relationships.

Questions:

1. What is your most comfortable presentation mode when addressing a group?

2. Has your experience in learning situations been mostly interactive or listening to lectures?

3. Do you learn best by listening to tapes? Interactive computer programs? Interacting with others?

4. When you need information, are you comfortable asking direct questions?

5. Are you slighted when someone doesn't readily accede to your experience?

6. Do you require a lot of detail and background when given a new assignment or directions?

7. Are you more comfortable receiving instructions from someone in your own age group?

8. Do you learn best by working things through? Being shown? Having things explained?

9. Are you most productive when left to your own devices? When working with others?

10. Do you multitask comfortably?

11. Do you prefer to stay focused on one thing at a time?

12. Are you "turned off" by long emails?

13. Do you typically work best alone, with a partner, or in a group?

14. Is there a group process with which you are most comfortable/uncomfortable?

Bursting Stereotypes

Resources abound to introduce you to or expand your knowledge about cultural backgrounds and stereotypes. As we all know, the stereotype is a basis for the multitude of exceptions. Think about the following whom you may have encountered personally: the New Yorker who isn't always in a hurry; the Southerner who is; the sensitive man and insensitive woman; the gentle football player and the brash musician. Those are just a few blatant examples. We all know people who defy stereotypes. Within your business and personal relationships, you see differences among the same and similarities among the different.

Team Activity: Create Your Own Culture

Bring together a team of six or more people. Give each person a large sheet of flip chart paper. Give the following instructions:

1. "For this exercise, write down the five attributes and characteristics that you believe most define you. Don't be shy; be honest. Don't identify yourself on the page."

2. Have participants tape their sheets in front of the room.

3. Now, have everyone form teams with those who have the most attributes in common.

4. The ideal: Based on the attributes identified, you will have created two or more teams. The outside possibility: Everyone is a match. That's okay, too.

5. Instruct each team to discuss the strengths they have as a team, based on the attributes identified.

6. Now, ask each team to identify those attributes and strengths that are missing.

7. Generate a discussion of the value of diverse, integrated teams.

Chapter

Change:
The Only Constant

"It's not the strongest of species that survive, nor the most intelligent, but the one
most responsive to change." —Charles
Darwin

▶ Change Is Life

▶ Finding Opportunities to Evolve

▶ Initiate the Change You See

▶ Who Is Tied to Your Change?

▶ Comfort Levels

▶ The Stress Response

Change Is Life

Change is an ever-present reality, an unavoidable reaction to being alive; part of life (and business) is being subject to change outside our control.

- The Earth is constantly changing.
- 98 percent of the atoms in your body are replaced every year.
  - Your skeleton is replaced every three months.
  - Your skin is replaced every four to five weeks.
  - You have a new stomach lining every four to five days.
  - Your liver is replaced every six weeks.
- Every moment is a moment that will never come again.

Adjusting Your Vision

Sometimes, a business grows and succeeds following a clear vision and then, someone blinks. Visions change, whether because of external or internal shifts; whether planned, based on looking ahead at market trends, or unplanned, because of sudden unexpected turns. How you handle and/or implement change will impact how well your team accepts and thrives through changes.

Figure 7.1: **SIX PRINCIPLES OF CHANGE**

1. Chance it. Nothing great was ever accomplished without risk. You cannot jump across a cavern in two small jumps; you have to leap. Look before you leap; calculate risks, but the other side of that canyon is not going to leap to you.

2. Harmonize. Changes flow more easily from a relaxed state of mind. Assess what is, determine what changes you want, set a reasonable time frame.

3. Anticipate. Think preemptively. What might be the next change in your industry? Your customer needs? Notice changes in your business and industry. What do you have to do to succeed in the new climate?

4. Network. Reach out, go to business functions, spread the word about your new direction or your choice to expand your team.

5. Generate. Initiate new ideas, and take action. Don't wait until everyone else in your industry has embraced the change and then jump on the bandwagon; lead the band.

6. Explore. Explore your options; explore what the competition is doing; brainstorm ideas for new angles; always be open to new possibilities.

Finding Opportunities to Evolve

Stop, look, and listen. Always be on the lookout for new opportunities. Anticipating that they will happen will make you more likely to see them when they do. Some opportunities are going to emerge as culture and technology evolve; some are already there. Electricity was not invented; it was harnessed.

The Internet is an example of an opportunity that was waiting for an entrepreneur.

We attended a conference about the Internet and its uses when the technology was in its infancy, maybe toddler stage. Thousands of products and services were available; however, tapping into them wasn't easy. The general reaction was: "Whoever can organize this mess will make a fortune." Enter Google, Ask Jeeves, and the birth of new concepts for the new technology, such as eBay's Internet auctions. Now, an Internet presence is regarded by most as a necessity. The fast integration of the Internet into everyday life as the place where people shop for services, local to global, and products from flowers to cars is a phenomenon that earlier generations never fathomed.

The Internet is on the superhighway of change. Marketing and traffic strategies change radically and often. If you're not taking full advantage of all the Internet has to offer, meet with an expert who can help you target the most efficient options to suit your needs. If you met with someone last year, it's time to reassess. Keep up, the best you can, with the exponential growth of opportunity.

As you plan your changes or expansion, keep your eye on the proverbial ball. Don't lose sight of your goal. As you assess opportunities, think through their relevance to your core business. Will they enhance or drain it?

QUICK Tip

Team wisdom:

"The future belongs to those who see possibilities before they become obvious."
—John Sculley, Former CEO of Pepsi and Apple Computers

InnovationEase: What can you learn about possible trends or product/service gaps from your customers? Once, while teaching a writing seminar, I suggested that class participants write down some key grammar and punctuation rules on index cards. "You should do that for us," suggested one young man. "You're absolutely right," I replied and Diamond Associates developed the Ease cards: PunctuEase™ and PronounEase™. Find out what customers are looking for; fill the gap.

Initiate the Change You See

Have you ever looked at one of those seemingly abstract illustrations with a clear picture embedded in it? Once you see the picture, you can't imagine how you missed it. If you are aware of your surroundings, your vision is likely to expand or change. If you are looking ahead, you will notice when industry changes and/or shifts in consumer priorities are on the horizon. Read the early signs and plan for the change—even be the first to try something on the cutting edge; yet, always carefully research the opportunities to minimize your risk.

What is going on in your external environment that can propel you to the next level?

Take stock of the business climate around you. What global, national, and/or industry changes will eventually trickle down to your business? What major issues and trends affect your organization? What can you do to be ready for change?

In their bestselling business book, *If It Ain't Broke, Break It*, Robert J. Kriegel and Louis Patler advise, "Move it before it moves you." Take this advice to heart. The world keeps on turning, and if you're not on the move by your own volition, forces outside of your control will move you. The perceptive business owner initiates change.

Be Prepared

We all know that change rarely happens when we are ready for it and some change can be a major setback. Even the best business people can be affected by events beyond their control. September 11 and Hurricane Katrina are all-too-graphic examples. Smaller ripples, such as a downturn in the economy, an election, a new discovery, or an old one that's suddenly obsolete, can affect individual businesses.

No one can be prepared for everything, but incorporate some change readiness in your business plan. Leave flexibility where you can in terms of budget and time frames; expect, as they say, the unexpected. Better yet, be the one to shake things up and you won't be caught off guard. Your ability to adapt to change can be the most important factor in moving your business forward.

Change, however, often comes with risk and, as romantic as it sounds to close your eyes and take a risk, using a solid risk/benefit assessment as a starting point for decision making is just good business. How do you assess a risk? That goes back to planning. How does this risk fit into your overall business plan? What is the cost of taking it and the cost of not? Don't pass up a short-term "tough patch" and miss long-term benefits. A simple pros and cons list is a good beginning for risk analysis.

Leadership Activity: Risk/Benefit Analysis

Chances are you've done this many times before. Think about a step you're contemplating. List the risks and benefits of going forward. Now, list the risks and benefits of not going forward.

Risks of Yes

_____

_____

_____

Risks of *No*

_____

_____

_____

Benefits of *Yes*

_____

_____

_____

Benefits of *No*

_____

_____

_____

Once you have completed the Risk/Benefit Analysis, explore options with your team, your accountant, and other advisors whom you trust. The least scientific and often final (and accurate) arbiter for the entrepreneur is "gut feeling." Once you make a decision, use your energy to implement. Don't distract by second-guessing. Do your questioning, fact-finding, and analysis up front. Then, go forth with confidence. The more effort you put into your plan up front, the easier the implementation.

Leadership Activity: The World Around You

Now, it is time to look at the world around you. What economic, business, and political factors and trends affect your business? Some have a positive effect; some a have a negative one. Think about how you can turn an external event or trend that is beyond your control into a business opportunity.

External Factors and Trends	Advantages	Disadvantages
•		
•		
•		
•		
•		
•		
•		

Look at the list that you created and brainstorm with your team to determine the potential challenges and the business opportunities they present. How can your team capitalize on opportunities? Can you find a business opportunity inherent in the disadvantages? Can you create one?

Figure 7.2: ISSUES AND TRENDS THAT AFFECT BUSINESS

- Revenue-related issues and trends
- Social and political value shifts
- Communication and information system trends
- Increased liability and risk management costs
- Increased emphasis on security

QUICK Tip

You don't have to be the early bird: Everyone knows the advantages of being the early bird. However, don't see others' early entry as your reason not to join in. Not being first has certain advantages, too. Often, you can learn from competitors' mistakes as they plunge ahead with a new product or service. Think of what would make you stand out. You may not be the first in line with the idea, but you can still be the first to present it with your unique style or to present an offer that will catch the eye of a prospective client or customer. Time to refine your plan may be more beneficial than being first.

Team Activity: Change Visions

Guide a roundtable discussion of ideas led by asking each team member the following questions in turn. Allow the group to discuss and build on new ideas.

- What very small step can you imagine that we might take, if our aim were to create an epidemic of positive change within our organization?

- If you had three wishes for our organization, what would they be? (Stated not as the absence of something, but stated positively as the presence of something.)

Set another meeting for following up on new ideas.

—Ronald Bell, Director, The Center for Business Excellence; ordained Presbyterian Minister and management consultant, Bridgewater, NJ

QUICK Tip

Know when to redirect your efforts: Savaradio's began as a small, upscale restaurant in Ventnor, a shore community adjacent to Atlantic City, New Jersey. Chef/owner Lisa Savage had an outstanding reputation and a strong following. During the peak summer season, her staff sometimes swelled to thirty. A neighborhood redevelopment project led a number of local businesses, including Savaradio's, to consider moving out. Lisa faced choices: sell the fixtures and get a job as a chef in another restaurant, relocate to another, similar site, or take the tiger by the tail and grow.

Lisa chose the latter, pulling together investors and planning to build a larger restaurant in Atlantic City, which had begun to attract a steadier stream of visitors and was close enough for the local regulars. But as plans took shape, Lisa monitored ongoing changes. Atlantic City, known primarily for gambling, with each casino offering a few high-end restaurants and a coffee shop, was suddenly exploding. The residents from neighboring communities, who used to patronize their local restaurants regularly, with an occasional casino restaurant night out, now found that the choices were increasing as hotels opened new restaurant and shopping plazas. On a cold winter night, dinner and shopping indoors with music in the background or going to a show or comedy club was more alluring for many than driving to the neighborhood restaurant.

Not afraid to change course, Lisa decided that a new, stand-alone upscale restaurant wasn't going to compete successfully with Atlantic City's new direction. She saw the draw of the casino plazas and anticipated the continuing trend. Lisa told her investors that she'd like to wait a bit and keep her eyes open. Now, having moved to a custom-designed facility in a new business complex in Linwood, a suburb outside of Atlantic City's shadow, Savaradio's is a magnet not only for its loyal followers and surrounding businesses, but for diners from the entire area and beyond.

Lisa's success is attributable to more than adaptability and foresight. She has also, through all transitions, had a clear understanding of what it takes to build a team (having started out as her own chef, shopper, and bookkeeper) and deep appreciation of her staff and advisors. "I try to surround myself with great people, many of them smarter than I am. I have a lot to learn." While she now has the freedom to spend her energies focused on management and teambuilding, she still works in the kitchen a few times a week. Savaradio's, which began as a small restaurant with five tables, now supports a staff of over one hundred.

Who Is Tied to Your Change?

Change is not vacuum-packed. When initiating change, keep in mind how your change affects others. Be sensitive to the comfort levels, learning curves, and associated changes of those around you. Information and involvement are the key factors to creating comfort in a change environment. Get the team's involvement and input at any stage possible and keep an open channel of communication for feedback and suggestions during transition periods.

Every change in our lives affects those connected to us. Following are some examples:

• You leave your 9–5 job and start your own business. You aren't as available to family, or even friends, as you used to be. Your children ask to see ID when you come home.

• You've been running your business with the same part-time support person for three years. The situation has been ideal for both of you. You pay what you can comfortably afford, and she has her afternoons off with her preschooler. You realize that with an increased client load (a good thing), you need full-time help. Full-time is not going to work for your current employee, and you can't afford two employees.

• Your business has grown successfully, and you've been approached by a competitor who would like to acquire it. For many reasons, the offer is appealing to you, but you have fifty employees who have been like family to you, all of whom will not be retained.

Think about how changes in others' lives have affected you and how changes in yours have affected others. Acknowledging the effect on others does not diminish the effect on you, nor does it mean that you should rethink the change. Knowing how others are touched by the change helps you assist them through the process. You cannot shoulder the responsibility for everyone who is connected to you on your path; however, recognizing the difficulty and opening their eyes to opportunity will help you all.

Many other business changes will result from team efforts and input. Working through changes with your team strengthens everyone's commitment and team members' bonds.

Leadership Activity: Ties

1. Brainstorm a list of business-related changes that you see on your immediate horizon.

2. Now, select the change that will have the greatest impact on you and write it in the center of a piece of paper. Think about everyone connected to you who will be impacted by that change, even slightly.

3. Think about how you can help each of these people through your change.

Team Activity: The Change Connection

1. In a seminar setting, ask for five volunteers.

2. Give them a long piece of ribbon (at least 1/2 inch wide) and have them stand side-by-side.

3. Have the volunteers hold the ribbon, end-to-end, wrapping it securely around their right hands.

4. Ask the person in the middle to start walking forward.

5. After about forty-five seconds, ask the five to stop.

6. Notice where each participant is. Discuss their reactions to the person moving forward. Some will have immediately followed, some will have stood their ground, others may have reluctantly been pulled along.

7. Now, facilitate a group discussion about the activity and how it may relate to those in the room.

The first time we conducted the Change Connection activity, the ribbon was too narrow, about 1/8 inch. When the lead person walked forward, one or two followed and some held their ground for dear life with the ribbon cutting into their hands. The discussion that followed about how much it hurt to stay back was beneficial to all. One participant, however, was totally shaken. She had been in limbo because the small company for which she had worked went out of business. She had not yet forgiven the business owner or moved on and was continually taking part-time work that held her back from moving forward in her career of choice. This exercise, she explained tearfully, put her resistance into perspective and she was ready to become fully engaged in taking the steps necessary to get her career back on track.

Figure 7.3: **FLOW THEORY**

Sometimes yielding is the strongest course, and strong teams know when to go with the flow. Some examples of flow in action:

- Think of the orchestra. If one player misses a note, the others must adapt and move forward. Being able to adapt to mistakes or changes is as important as learning the score.

- Sailors know how dangerous it is to make a hard turn against the current. It takes an understanding of external forces—the currents and the relationship between those currents, the sail, and the boat itself—to safely maneuver the changing tides.

- Surfers position themselves to ride the wave, aligned with its power.

The tides of business are ever-changing. Are you ready to ride?

Comfort Levels

What's your comfort level with change? What about your team members?

Many consider change stressful. The proliferation of change and stress management workshops is testament to the overwhelming effects of change in the workplace and beyond. However, is it really change that causes the stress? Is it the new plan, the unexpected turns of a project, the team member who is suddenly coming in with radical ideas? Or is it our reactions to the new plan, the new unexpected turns of a project, the team member who is suddenly coming in with radical ideas?

It may be true that the plan seems impossible, the unexpected turns make the job more difficult, and the radical ideas sound ridiculous, but stressing out or stewing only takes more energy that would be used more wisely toward adapting to the situation at hand. And any of these things has a potential to expand your knowledge and experience. If you wonder whether it's really possible to control your stress or true that your reaction is the key to minimizing stress, consider this question: Is everyone in the same circumstance under the same amount of stress over it? Of course not! The difference is, more often than not, as simple (and as complex) as outlook.

What Stresses You?

We all have things that push our stress buttons. Realizing what those things are is the first step toward taking control of our stress. Stress can also be a warning sign, a gut instinct; if stress is not your normal reflex, it may be telling you to slow down or think again.

The perpetual naysayer can bring down the team, but healthy skepticism should be welcome. The team member hesitant to make a change may be most likely to come up with objections that will help you hone the plan, avoid pitfalls, or reevaluate. Everyone's perspective has value. All you can do is encourage team members not to rush to judgment.

If you stress over change, the team exercise Change Is… would be interesting for you to work through with your team.

Team Activity: Change Is...

Step 1: Have each team member write true or false by each of the ten statements below. Then open a team discussion.

1. Change is bad.

2. Change is frightening.

3. Change is threatening.

4. Change is good.

5. Change is exciting.

6. Change is tiresome.

7. Change is troublesome.

8. Change is necessary, if only to shake things up.

9. Change is a sign of order breaking down.

10. Change is a sign of progress.

Step 2: Point out (or reinforce the point if it has been discussed), that none of these statements is inherently true. The only thing that can be said about all change is that, good or bad, change is a necessary part of life. Though not always, sometimes a change that seems negative at first can, in the long run, be a good thing.

Step 3: Ask team members to share instances in which a change that looked daunting turned out to be positive.

Follow-up questions:

1. What was the cause of the resistance?

2. How much stress did worrying cause?

3. What would have been the worst-case scenario?

4. Were relationships unnecessarily damaged or tested?

The Stress Response

As change sets off a stress reaction for so many, understanding that response is important. When someone has what seems to be an extreme reaction to change, realize that often the response is automatic and physiological. When under stress, our bodies go into "fight or flight" mode—prepared to either run or fight. This primitive response was designed to save us from physical harm, but these days, much of our stress is about ego survival. If you are the one suffering from stress, you have the choice to take on the task of retraining your brain; if others' stress is the issue, do what you can to minimize that stress and avoid surprises whenever possible.

So what happens when the stress response hits? Your heart is racing, blood pressure soaring, blood sugar rising, digestion of that breakfast bagel or heavy lunch has virtually stopped, and your whole body is pumped for action. In classic cartoon style, steam is coming out of your ears and your hair is standing on end. Nature would also have your brain become defensive, scanning your enemy for weakness, and keenly focused on "survival." The good news: if you are in danger, your body functions will alter to give you the capacity for greater strength, agility, and speed. The bad news: Your body doesn't know the difference between a lion and a sudden shift that pushes your deadline up a week. So now, your body is geared to run hard or fight for your life. You've been fully prepared for a physical response, but the appropriate response isn't to fight or to run through the office, jumping over desks. The question becomes: what does one do in civilization with survival mechanisms designed for physical survival in the wild?

What happens to most people in the absence of stress coping or stress reduction mechanisms is illness. Chronic stress affects the heart, the immune system, and the brain. Finding coping mechanisms is not only good for business, it's good for health.

Be aware of your reactions. Put some of your stress energy, as it arises, towards accepting that change is constant and developing a mindset and tools to live in an evolving environment. Tools, for you, may include any sort of relaxation or meditation techniques, anything that feels, for you, like "blowing off steam," any process that helps you better understand the change in a way that will add to your comfort level.

Figure 7.4: FIGHT OR FLIGHT

Physical Response	Nature's Purpose
Heart speeds up and blood pressure rises	Allows increased flow of blood to the brain to help you think fast when in a position to make life-and-death choices
Digestion is slowed	Blood is shunted away from the gut for increased muscle strength
Blood sugar rises	Provides more fuel for energy
Breathing becomes rapid	Allows the lungs to take in more oxygen
Immune system function is impaired	Redistributes infection fighters
Fluids are diverted from the mouth	Causes dryness and difficulty in talking; spasms of the throat muscles can make it difficult to swallow
Blood flow is diverted from the skin	To support the heart and muscle tissues, making skin cool and clammy; also causes the scalp to tighten, which is where we get the image of someone's hair "standing on end"

Warn of impending changes: Change is scary. People generally fear change. Do you or others around you silently consider alternatives and then, without any warning, suddenly ask others to implement them? It's the organizational equivalent of someone popping up and yelling "BOO!" in a darkened room.

—Rochelle Deveraux, owner, Business Efficacy, Salem, OR, www.businessmasters.com

QUICK Tip

Embrace the unexpected: The Edward Lowe Foundation was hosting a retreat for a group of women business owners at its headquarters on 2,500 acres of forest woods and farmlands. In addition to being project manager, I was cofacilitating the session. This retreat was the kick-off event for our retreat season. It was also this organization's first visit to the property, and I wanted them to have a remarkable experience.

A cornerstone activity of our program is the Reflective Walk, which consists of six separate contemplation areas along a gorgeous nature trail—plus a series of thought-provoking questions. Key to the walk is silence. My cofacilitator, Eric, took the group out to the trail. As I followed, soon after, I could hear a loud mechanical grinding noise approaching. We had the property to ourselves—it was a Saturday morning. So what was that noise?

I could see the entire group of women standing at the top of the first hill looking down and to the left at the approaching noise. They should be further along, I thought, but the noise was staggering. "What the heck is that?" a voice in my brain screamed just as a large vehicle, with ten-foot high wheels, was passing in front of the group. It made an awful roar as it pulled a large tree past the women.

Eric calmly took the women on to the next stopping point as I raced after the vehicle while calling the property manager. I stopped the driver just as he was turning for the return trip back down the hill toward my group. Our property manager reported that the tree cutters were supposed to have done this job earlier in the week but had shown up unannounced that morning. I insisted that they shut down for about thirty minutes and hustled back thinking, "Oh boy— this could be bad."

The group was working quietly on the first series of questions when I rejoined them. "But oh just wait for the debrief," I thought. Reflective Walk indeed—all except for an industrial size logging truck breaking into our serene contemplative setting. I was already rehearsing my apologies.

But when Eric asked what they thought of the walk (the general question we ask to initiate conversation), an amazing thing happened. The first participant said: "As I was standing there looking at the truck pulling that tree up the hill, I was thinking of my business. I think that I am that tree—being dragged away. I am out of control." "Can it be," I thought, "a metaphor has been found and used? How brilliant!"

The next woman to speak added, "And I saw the rut that the tree left behind— and that's me right now." Absolutely amazing—the group found comparisons and thought starters from an unplanned event. To this day I am reminded to expect the unexpected during all facilitated events involving human beings. Now if I could only arrange for the logger to come by at each event!

—Dino Signore, program manager for the Edward Lowe Foundation, MI, edwardlowe.org, and principal owner of the Sherpa Group consulting firm

Chapter

The Virtual Team

"The global reach of the Internet and the anonymity of email can, at times, make it tempting to treat individuals haphazardly, almost as disposable commodities. We're all just words on a page, or pixels on a screen to each other. But the importance of human relationships must remain paramount." —Steve Lefkowitz, entrepreneur

▶ The Technological Boardroom

▶ Building Trust

▶ Information Sharing

▶ Communication Etiquette

▶ The Virtually Invisible Team Member

The Technological Boardroom

Once upon a time (and not so long ago), it was widely believed that a strong team bond could only be formed in person. Now, with the myriad of distance communication options—cell phones, email, instant messaging, collaboration software, online calendars and scheduling, online meeting forums and webinars, online bulletin boards, video conferencing, discussion forums, and more—a team can be scattered throughout the globe and still in the same "room." Legions who once swore never to give in to computers are now Internet savvy, and each progressive generation has started on computers younger and younger, often creating relationships worldwide as though it's the most natural course.

Virtual Reality

The physical conference room and suite of offices, for many businesses, are options but no longer necessities. Many teams, in a wide array of industries, are exclusively virtual, with little or no face-to-face interaction. Others maintain a central hub, but employ off-site team members both in-state and out, and in or out of the country.

From fully virtual to one or two virtual team members to in-house team members going virtual a few days per week—all options are viable as long as they work for you. You can also choose whether you want to be seen as a virtual office or create the illusion of having a large physical base of operations. Many virtual offices create a brick and mortar façade by using virtual off-site receptionists who are ready to answer basic questions, send you messages via phone or email, and sound as though they're right there in your buzzing office.

The virtual team, like any other, goes through stages of team development and is no stranger to the storming aspect as conflict, role confusion, and process or style debates emerge. Also, just as any team, virtual teams need clear roles, structure, process, communication channels, and systems of perks and rewards. Do what you can to create and maintain a sense of team. For example, giving logoed gadgets, widgets, and screen savers brings a sense of team culture into remote and home offices.

Virtual commuting is a win/win situation for many employers and self-starting, motivated employees. However, the arrangement may not be for everyone. If you have a team member who would like to go virtual, try it first, if possible, on a limited basis. Check in, leave room for adjustment time (to technical difficulties, interpersonal changes, scheduling bumps, relationship reframing, and the inevitable initial setbacks) without being quick to give up or discourage. Leave the door open, though, for a supportive return if the system isn't working out.

QUICK Tip

Creating a Web presence: "Going virtual" is not an all or nothing choice. By embracing technology and the endless options it offers, business owners can expand their reach farther than ever before. A company website extends not only your visibility and accessibility to clients and customers, but opens doors to opportunities to network with colleagues worldwide. Virtual business realities are for everyone, not only those with computer-based businesses. You can draw attention to your business through your website, blogging (posting regular messages on a company blog), linking to and from partners, and even attending virtual trade fairs, which put the small business owner in touch with large corporations with the click of a mouse.

Alert!

Find what's best for you and your team: Virtual teams are all around you. The book in your hand is a product of virtual teamwork. We used to work side-by-side and the synergy was smooth and easy. When we transitioned to virtual teamwork, we faced a myriad of technical challenges. We were also often frustrated by the feeling that we would work more easily if we were in a room together with the book in front of us, passing pages and feeling the energy in the room as we shared ideas. By the time we had the opportunity to see each other, we thought a "working" visit would be uplifting and highly productive. What a team! We were awful. While visiting was fun, when it came to work, we were stifling each other. We both needed more space for the creative process and couldn't wait to get back to our distance teamwork arrangement. In the end, we made the virtual shift, and it works well.

What's the moral? We have no idea. To us, it's sort of a mystery of human dynamics. What we do know is that synergy returned when we were in our respective states, and the process feels lighter now that we no longer have the nagging "grass is greener" feeling, remembering what it was like to work in the same space. Of course, back then we had trouble with office distractions and untimely snow shutdowns in winter. If there is a moral to this story, maybe that's it. If you think the grass is greener outside the virtual environment, maybe your monitor just needs a color adjustment; working side-by-side has its challenges, too.

Building Trust

Trust, virtual or otherwise, must be earned. While shaking hands is a first step that cannot be virtually achieved, building trust from a distance is possible. While all teams need ground rules and clear expectations, establishing and following these basic agreements is key to trust-building on a virtual team.

Virtual team members who don't have the benefit of face-to-face time during "business hours," need to feel connected and confident that other team members or team leaders are taking care of their responsibilities as they relate to the whole team effort. Tensions run high when someone is out of touch as deadlines are bearing down. Understanding schedules, expectations, and operating within agreed upon frameworks helps everyone function with greater ease, comfort, and efficiency.

Certain protocols, which are important in any office, become indispensable among virtual colleagues. Up-front agreements on communication processes—and adherence to those processes—increases comfort and trust.

Establish a time frame for acknowledging emails and requests. Fulfilling requests might take longer, but no team member should go more than twenty-four hours without knowing whether the request was received. A compulsive email checker who is working with someone who checks three times a day can become frustrated and believe that messages are being ignored. Lack of response leaves people wondering if (or assuming that) their requests are being back-burnered, resented, or simply not received.

Figure 8.1: **TRUST BUILDERS**

- Establish clear, agreed upon expectations.
- Attend to needs.
- Respond to emails in an appropriate time frame.
- Set and maintain a positive tone.
- Own up to mistakes.
- Copy all parties who would expect to be (or appreciate being) in the loop.
- Create or discuss—up front—policies regarding copying and blind copying communications.
- Determine "check in" times that work for everyone.
- Meet expectations.
- Follow through.

Knowing the Team

We also like to "know whom we're dealing with." Take time up front for introductions, and establish a way for new members to be introduced to the group and for the group to introduce themselves to the new member. Have a space online where team member bios and/or photos are posted. It helps, even in this virtual world of ours, to put a human face to the voice or words on a screen.

Real-life-style interactions and keeping up with team members build trust, as well. Send bulletins highlighting member accomplishments and allow members to share exciting "what's new" moments. Provide electronic "water coolers" in the form of chat rooms or discussion boards.

Team Activity: Communication Profile

The following is helpful when establishing expectations for a virtual team. As new team members arrive, ask them their positions and consider whether expectations should be revised.

- What do you consider a reasonable response time for acknowledging requests?

- If a message is not marked "urgent," how quickly would you expect a response?

- Are you on your email all day, or do you check in at certain times?

- Do you check your email on the weekend?

- How can you be reached if a matter is urgent?

- Is there a typical situation in which you would prefer a call to an email?

QUICK Tip

Know your market: Before we started our business, MyTherapyNet.com, I had a grand vision—to deliver mental health services via the Internet. A simple premise that was globally scalable. We started the company in April of 2000—just after the dot-com bubble burst. While therapists were calling me crazy to think that therapy could be performed online, investors were calling me crazy for starting an Internet business when "the Internet was over."

Being surrounded by such negativity actually greatly helped to provide a very clear action plan that addressed what I had to accomplish before even getting started. I knew two things—1) although Internet stocks were a terrible investment, people were signing on to the Internet in ever-increasing numbers. 2) using the written word in therapy (journaling is a very common and effective therapeutic tool) could be highly effective for some mental issues. Neither of these points could be reasonably contested.

The key was to assemble a team of experts in each of the areas to successfully create a foundation on which to build the technology I envisioned: a virtual office building for the licensed mental health practitioner. We would provide an environment that afforded anonymity, convenience, and security to anyone wishing to seek mental help.

This meant pulling together experts in psychology, law, business, technology, and education. Once I had our team in place, we discussed and addressed every possible objection to our endeavor. We knew that there were answers to every objection because the end result of providing online therapy as an option for people in need was certain to have merit. We conducted research, retained consultants, and left no question unaddressed.

Once we determined the lay of the land, we were then able to make what, looking back, have proven to be the right choices. And these "right choices" boil down to a set of principles upon which we built this business. Remarkably, the first team we created built the team that has managed the exponential growth of our company over the past six years. Assembling multiple minds to make the "right choices" certainly gave our "revolutionary" idea the best chance at success.

—Kathleene Derrig-Palumbo, PhD, CEO My Therapy Net, Inc., mytherapynet.com

Information Sharing

Develop a protocol for sharing information. Everyone on the team should be in the habit of sending messages that clearly state the purpose, what is needed in return and when. A clear subject line is essential so that the recipient knows what has come in and can find the email later, if necessary.

Keep communications in a shared database. Email provides valuable documentation of how issues were resolved and stages that were determined and executed, which may not be written down anywhere else. This email trail can be useful in looking back on a project and creating guidelines and standards for future projects. The email trail is also helpful for new team members coming in.

Sharing schedules, project timelines, and progress charts is especially useful for remote team members. Calendars with critical meeting and deadline dates should be accessible to everyone. Vacation or business travel dates should also be marked in advance so everyone on the team can schedule questions and requests accordingly.

Information sharing and collaboration software can streamline your processes, allowing shared files, even the ability to see each others' desktops and work in the same file at the same time. The technology for collaborative working is widespread, beyond highly-specialized collaboration software.

Posting to the Web

Wikis are websites especially designed for collaboration where users can freely edit content. In some cases, users must be registered (and registration may or may not be restrictive), but some are simply wide-open forums. (wiki software programs allow for any of these options.) These sites offer easy access to html code, allowing user changes to site content to appear immediately online.

If you are unfamiliar with wikis, look at the online user-collaborative free encyclopedia at wikipedia.org. Search for a topic of interest, and, if you know something more about it or see misinformation, click the edit tab and make your changes. You can view the history of changes and discussions of those free agents who choose to contribute their knowledge to the site. You can also start your own page. As you might imagine, wikis have their vandals, but those who care about the subject of a page monitor additions (though you might not want to rely heavily on the facts on a wiki that's open to anyone's edits).

In larger companies, blogs (weblogs) are used both internally and externally. Company executives will choose the casual, dependable, "personal" style of a blog to "speak" to employees. An executive blog may also be directed to the public; most often the task of creating and maintaining a blog is delegated to a team member or members. Blogs, unlike the corporate image projected by your website, are designed to have a more casual tone and sound more like a friendly letter than a corporate staff writer. Let your personality speak for itself and encourage your team members to do the same.

Your blog can have your company's latest news, links to related news, your thoughts on that news, updates, customer feedback, photos of interest, or anything that would be of ongoing relevance. It's your blog; have fun and your customers (or potential customers) will too. If employees want to run blogs on your company's topic, establish guidelines to protect proprietary information, but allow some creative reign.

A blog can be a great ongoing team activity, with multiple team members posting at different times. Team members can decide what goes into your blog. If you or your team commit to a blog, stick to it or hire someone else who can. If people like your blog, they'll check in regularly—until you go a few weeks without updating.

Communication Etiquette

Email

Phones have the advantage of offering some social cues. We can hear tone of voice and even smiles. The human spirit was quick, online, to find a way to emote through email messages by creating smiles :) winks ;) even surprise =:o and these emoticons, silly as they may seem, can clarify the tone of a message. Messages often have so many possible interpretations. A subtle joke or lighthearted sarcasm can unwittingly create deep resentment when just a few little punctuation marks can let people know we're on their side and smiling. Even with emoticon's simplistic simulations, in the absence of the visible smile—or quizzical look—your language by email must be clear, concise, and unambiguous. Forget the little joke if it might be misunderstood. Just be clear. Be aware, as well, of the tonal messages of email and don't SHOUT by using all capital letters.

Message Response Time

Maybe you don't have time to answer the email or voice mail immediately. If you know the email sender sits on pins and needles or will soon be unavailable, at the very least, shoot back a "Thanks, I'll get back to you tomorrow" note. As for the phone call, if you can call back within a reasonable time frame, call back when you can talk, but if the call is expected or the caller needs to at least know when you will be available to talk, return the call just to touch base and plan a time. It's a courtesy call, but be firm about when you can speak and don't get trapped when you're under time pressure. In fact, if someone else can return the call for you, all the better.

The Rolling Present

Some contact may be real-time, but varied schedules, and often time zones, can have people working in what's known as the "rolling present." This term comes from team technologies that do not operate in real time, such as email, discussion boards, listservs, and aspects of conferencing software. A team's schedule could leave someone signing in and finding "new" posts or advancements hours later; if this person just logged in, the latest post (even if it was twelve hours ago), is considered "current." As long as everyone understands team member schedules, this virtual reality can work smoothly. However, some problems inherent in the rolling present may be difficult to address.

If most team members have access all day long to a discussion board, they may sign on a number of times, hammer out an issue, and feel it's largely resolved. The team members who cannot sign on until much later, because of time zones or a schedule that involves being out with clients all day, may be seen as "rehashing" from the first moment they have to chime in. To avoid this problem, team members may want to slow the pace of discussing non-time-sensitive issues or, at least, be very clear that all members must have a chance, within a reasonable turnaround time, to chime in.

Conferencing

Do your best to be in a quiet location without distractions. A landline is preferable to a connection that might cut out, but do what you can. Have the best equipment for your purposes in the central location. Productivity will be hindered if team members are frustrated by the sound quality of a speakerphone.

If some are in the room and others are on the phone, those in remote locations are at a disadvantage. Often, we do not have long pauses between speakers, but nonverbal cues that point to an opening to speak. Inject deliberate pause time to ask those on the phone if they have anything to add. On the other hand, a speaker pausing to think may be clear to those in the room but not those on the phone. Allow for the understanding that interruptions are often inadvertent, due to limited personal cues.

Whether Web conferencing or teleconferencing, meeting preparation is especially essential when people won't be in the same room. Distribute meeting agendas ahead of time. Also distribute any other materials that might prove helpful to give team members additional "think" time prior to the meeting.

Technical transitions: When adding, streamlining, or upgrading team technology, leave time in the schedule for training and the inevitable bugs in the system (whether caused by technical problems or time required for the learning curve). Team members less familiar with computers should have a focused initial orientation to increase their comfort levels and increase their baseline knowledge. Test new equipment; transition before trashing the old. When considering what equipment you need, think of compatibility and creating room for growth and expansion. At the same time, you'll find that if you buy high-tech, complex equipment for low-tech, overworked people, the technology, not to mention a lot of money, will probably be wasted.

The Virtually Invisible Team Member

In some cases, one or just a few team members are based in satellite locations. Your brick and mortar team must learn to function as virtual teams do and to remember that off-site colleagues are still part of the team.

- Invite the off-site member(s) to meetings via conference calls.
- Do not make office announcements without putting them in writing and sending to all team members.
- Create teams within the team that pair off-site/on-site team members, making the on-site responsible for keeping off-site partners in the loop. What can seem like a passing comment in the office might be packed with critical information.

Give as much attention to those team members who are not in your location as you do to those you see every day. "Out-of-sight-out-of-mind" doesn't boost morale or strengthen your team. Be careful of giving a disproportionate amount of your extra time, bonuses, perks, and opportunities to those who are in your physical space. Obviously, this will leave team members feeling isolated, unmotivated, discouraged, and devalued. Attitudes toward the "invisible" team member affect morale, productivity, and the functioning of the whole team.

Bringing the "Outsiders" In

Those in the office may have a sense of virtual commuters as slackers or believe they're getting away with something. The "insiders" may feel put upon by requests from those outside the office, resentful that they don't seem to understand the urgency of other matters in the office. These feelings can lead to treating the telecommuter as the "outsider" whose every teamwork request is handled as though he or she is asking for a favor. They may judge someone who's at a child's soccer game in the middle of the afternoon as an uncommitted worker, even if the cell phone is on and that person has been on evening conference calls with people in a different time zone for three days running.

Virtual commuters need to be judged on availability, as agreed upon with the team, as well as output. In many situations, work styles and the time of the day or night that they get things done is irrelevant as long as they are meeting team deadlines. In other cases, when back-and-forth contact or the need to get the answer when the question arises is paramount, those off-site have very clear parameters. Ensure that guidelines are reasonable, consistent, and shared. An employee, who previously worked as a virtual team member for a "just-get-the-job-done" company, needs to know that your company is one that expects 9–5 availability from everyone at every location.

Off-site team members are a part of your organization and should not be relegated to the hinterlands of your team. Additional effort may be required to make them feel part of the team. Everyone should be clear that the effort is important; as always, the teamwork attitude begins with you. Do what you can to create and maintain everyone's sense of team, from clear communication to sending logoed gadgets and screen savers to bring a sense of team culture into remote offices. Start, though, by making clear that out-of-site doesn't mean out-of-mind, and just because virtual team members cannot be seen, doesn't mean they aren't substantial, integral members of your team.

QUICK Tip

Know your time zones: You may have to think and operate in two or more time zones. Adjustment may be difficult at first. Think about how your communication choices can work for your team.

- Schedule telephone calls, webinars, and video conferencing far enough in advance to ensure everyone's availability. Someone may have to be present significantly earlier or later than normal business hours.

- Consider others' time zones when sending email, requesting a review, response, or information.

- If your team is on a tight deadline and you have a limited real-time zone overlap, hold that time sacred whenever possible and be accessible. Be clear about where and how you can be reached.

Figure 8.2: **WHY GO VIRTUAL?**

Good for employers:

- Saves money in real estate costs: Even just scaling down your physical operation saves money.

- Saves money by aiding in retention: Retraining costs money; allowing for the work-at-home option increases team members feeling appreciated, trusted, and rewarded. You will also be able to retain team members who move or have life changes that require scaling back or putting in the required time at odd hours.

- Increases your pool of potential team members: When people can work with you from anywhere, you broaden your scope of available talent.

- Improves recruiting: People are increasingly aware of virtual possibilities. Knowing that some level of flexibility is an option makes your organization more inviting.

- Increases productivity: Study after study shows that productivity increases. Theories include: less stress from commuting, lower overall stress (which improves morale and decreases absenteeism), feelings of empowerment, and desire to overcome the misperception that being home means slacking off.

- Provides a stable "headquarters": The virtual office is less vulnerable and quicker to recover in the face of blizzards, hurricanes, and earthquakes.

- Motivates employees: Virtual commuting is good for couples, families, and overall stress reduction. What makes your team members happy and healthy is good for you.

- Conserves the energy—both fuel and human—burned in commuting.

- Offers potential tax incentives: Ask your accountant about potential tax incentives that have been put in place to help businesses capitalize on the environmental and social benefits of virtual commuting.

- Good for the environment and global warming trends: Fewer people commuting on the roads leads to lowered pollution levels and less carbon dioxide in the air.

QUICK Tip

Treat your virtual employees as you would like to be treated: I recently started a design business from my home. Rather than rush my business launch and risk attracting many new clients that I may have had trouble serving, I decided to take a more cautious approach. I delayed the launch of my business and took time to build a solid team of graphic design subcontractors. I advertised for artists in my Sunday paper, and the ad also appeared on the paper's website. I received three hundred resumes. I was overwhelmed and needed a management strategy fast. I used my existing client work already in the pipeline as a means to test and train my eager new freelance team.

How would I decide? For obvious reasons, it was clear that my first contact with these three hundred strangers who wanted something from me would have to be a "mass mailing." I invited all of them to take an online skills test, imploring each of them to take no longer than a half hour to read the instructions and go through the steps of a web-based test I had quickly put together. This was a very effective tool.

Of my three hundred applicants, only about three dozen took the test. A few were grateful they had been elevated to the testing round. And a few had some very creative suggestions as to what I could do with my online test. Such language! And because they had, without knowing it, as a group, decided for me who among them would be easiest to work with, I was grateful...so I gave back to them by quickly designing a "test results" website where I critiqued the entries, which also created a sense of community by allowing them to see each other's work.

I think it was this step of the process that convinced everyone involved, even me, that more than "hiring help," I was building a team. In the end, I gathered up all the completed assignments delivered to me electronically and assembled them into a finished job. I took the step of paying all my freelancers out of an initial deposit I'd received on the job, rather than waiting for my client to pay me the balance.

Each and every freelancer said they'd work for me again. Some said I was the best client they'd ever worked for. I didn't hire any of them for more than $250 worth of work, so this enthusiasm was based entirely on how I'd treated them simply through the tone of my emails and my commitment to treating them how I wish I'd been treated by clients throughout my career.

Epilogue

After all my designers delivered their completed work to my email inbox, I had to ask them to send me their social security numbers so that I could pay them. Some insisted on a phone call. No problem. But one guy, after doing beautiful work and always delivering on time, said he couldn't give me his social security or tax ID number. He apologized, but explained that because he lives in Australia he doesn't have either one. Australia! The guy had seen my online ad, put himself through my entire interview process, done all the work and never once let on that he was more than say, a few towns over!

—Steve Lefkowitz, Founder/Publisher, Pen at Work, Philadelphia, PA, www.penatwork.com

Finding activities for your virtual team: No, you can't go jumping out of planes together or even to a company picnic, but many of the team activities in this book can be adapted to online forums, and "think" sessions can still be facilitated, either with instant messaging, more advanced conferencing software, or through a discussion in the "rolling present" through emails or discussion boards. You and your team can still put your heads together, from any distance.

QUICK Tip

Find a way to celebrate: Celebrate accomplishments with your team. Just because they are not colocated doesn't mean that they can't celebrate together. If you can have team members in the same town for a project's kick-off, wind up, or at interim points, do it. If that isn't feasible, maintain a focus on noting milestones and delineating clear beginnings and ends to projects. Show appreciation; give positive feedback and thanks online, in discussion groups, in a blog, or copied to the team and anyone else who would enjoy sharing the sense of accomplishment. Just because you're not in the same room doesn't mean you can't share a toast, blow off some steam, and laugh about the hurdles that made you say, "We'll laugh about that some day."

Chapter

Periodic Inventory

"If we did all the things we were capable of doing, we would literally astound ourselves." —Thomas Edison

▶ Taking Stock

▶ Personnel

▶ Product/Service Assessment

▶ Your Stakeholders

▶ Take Care of Your Team

Taking Stock

Without periodic review of your strategic plan, processes, and human and capital resources, you cannot build your team and your business wisely. How well does your team function to achieve your company's vision and meet its goals? Typically, those who run small businesses focus on sales and marketing, customer service and satisfaction, and product development and enhancement. What they tend to ignore is making time to review how they are doing and how to improve the way the business functions.

You may have started with a business plan, or, like many entrepreneurs, you jumped right in and began a business with the potential to thrive and grow. Now is the time to take stock before charging ahead. A key tool for taking stock is the SWOT (Strengths, Weaknesses, Opportunities, and Threats) Analysis. This exercise gives a broad perspective of factors, both internal and external, that impact the growth and direction of your business.

Involve Your Team

As you explore, have your team brainstorm to complete the "How Are We Doing?" team activity (pages 178–179). Depending upon your business's size and structure, you may conduct this as a team-of-the-whole activity, small group activities that then come together to share, or department activities.

Often, a company leader or a business owner asks for input, generates a great deal of activity and discussion, creates a buzz of excitement brought on by the anticipation of change at some level, and then returns to "business as usual." Those who enthusiastically shared and delved and created and problem-solved become more disillusioned than they might have been if no discussion had ever been generated. In some companies, disenchanted employees refer to each new initiative as "the flavor of the month."

Once you engage your team to take stock, you have a responsibility to hear what they come up with and to consider their recommendations. If you don't, you will create a sense of mistrust and inertia. Many ideas will surface: some realistic, some not. Look at what is possible, affordable, and attainable within a short, realistic time frame. You do not have to be the one to take the action. Delegate to one or more team members. Chances are, they will welcome the responsibility and the opportunity to effect change.

Preempt Problems

Taking stock is often brought on by an event: an unhappy client, a situation that didn't work out as planned, or a dispute that shows you everyone wasn't as clear as you had thought. Be sure that everyone on your team has the same quality standards and the same beliefs about customer care. If you are working with a supplier or manufacturer who has different ideas about quality or service than you do, your clients will lose faith in you. If you are caught between an unhappy customer and a supplier who won't budge, reevaluate your supplier. One way to preempt problems is to recognize when a business relationship is not working to you or your client's advantage and move on.

A good time to take stock is after a particularly challenging or stressful project or series of events. How did we complicate the situation? How can we better prepare for the next onslaught? Don't play the blame game. Pull together all critical team members and really look at what happened:

- What went wrong?
- What was the cause?
- What was the result?
- Is a salvage plan in order? If so, that's Step 1.
- What processes need repair?
- What directions could be clearer?
- What lines of authority got tangled?
- What's coming up that could hit the same snag? Have an action plan in place to prevent that.
- What changes must be made in:
  - Communication
  - Behavior
  - Equipment
  - Planning
  - Chain of responsibility

Don't bat these ideas around, adjourn, and wait for the next shoe to drop. Assign responsibility and initiate change.

Leadership Activity: SWOT Analysis

Answer the following questions in each category, then think of additional SWOT statements specific to you and your business.

To gain an even broader picture, once you complete the SWOT Analysis, run through it again as though you are one of your competitors. Obviously, you will have less inside information on this perspective, but flipping the point of view to another business owner with a different set of apparent strengths and weaknesses might give you some interesting insights.

Keep your answers short, simple, specific, and realistic.

Strengths:

- What is your strongest business asset?
- Do you consider your team strong? Why?
- What do you offer that makes you stand out from the rest?
- What unique resources do you have?
- Do you have any special marketing expertise?
- Do you have a broad customer base?
- Additional strengths:

Weaknesses:

- What can be improved?
- In what areas do your competitors have the edge?
- What necessary expertise/manpower do you currently lack?
- Do you have cash flow problems?
- Are you relying primarily on just a few clients or customers?
- Additional weaknesses:

Opportunities:

- What trends do you see in your industry?
- What trends do you foresee?
- What trends might impact your industry?

- What external changes present interesting opportunities?
- What have you seen in the news recently that might present an opportunity?
- Additional opportunities:

Threats:

- What obstacles do you face?
- What is the competition doing that you're not?
- What challenges can be turned into opportunities?
- Are external economic forces affecting your bottom line?
- Additional threats:

Did you consider...?

The following might be strengths or weaknesses for you. If you have not included them in your SWOT Analysis, consider if—and where—they should be added:

- Location
- Web presence
- Company image
- Quality
- Service
- Pricing

The following are additional items to consider, if you haven't, as potential opportunities or threats:

- Price wars
- Technology shifts
- Mergers (your or a competitor's merger opportunities, plans, or progress)
- Joint ventures (your or a competitor's joint venture opportunities, plans, or progress)

Team Activity: How Are We Doing?

Give the following instructions to your team, or split your team into small groups and reconvene after they are finished with the assessment:

Step 1: Work as a team to complete the questions below.

Step 2: Review these lists and refine them. Determine priorities and emergencies.

Step 3: Consider how to build on the positive and overcome the negative.

Step 4: Determine those items your team has the authority and power to change and those that would require your attention.

Step 5: Share your decisions with the team.

Step 6: Establish an action plan assigning specific time frames and responsibilities.

Part 1: What's working for us?

1. What are we doing well? correctly? successfully?

-
-
-
-
-
-
-
-

2. What about our team (people, resources, mindsets, behaviors) contributes to our ability to achieve the above?

-
-
-
-
-
-
-

Part 2: What can we improve?

How do we, as a team, get in our own way?

What equipment and/or processes are obsolete?

What mindsets and/or resources are counterproductive?

How can we improve staffing?

How can we improve training?

Are our products/services keeping pace with market demand?

QUICK Tip

The importance of goals and teamwork: A strong team culture defines an organization. I first joined Selecto-Flash, a forty-five-year old company, five years ago. Established and managed by a salesperson, the company functioned as a job shop geared to "get the job out." Many business decisions were impulsive reactions to opportunities, and team members were focused on their responsibilities only. While a caring management created a sense of family and inspired customer loyalty by meeting needs at any cost, something was missing. We realized that a culture shift could give Selecto-Flash a much-needed boost.

We also knew change would be difficult for some and would take considerable time. Our process took into consideration the need for gradual change; we embarked on the slow, deliberate journey from a workforce driven by moment-to-moment priorities to a cohesive unit working together to achieve company goals and successes. The shift began with creating a company vision, setting achievable, measurable goals, and listening to the valuable input of all employees.

Our company has turned around from significant losses to increased profits each year, doubling revenue in four years. Selecto-Flash continues to grow as a result of the enthusiasm and participation of the entire staff working together. We truly have achieved a team-driven culture without losing the valuable emphasis on quality, timely products, and outstanding customer service.

The change is apparent not only in the bottom line, but in the camaraderie of the group and the pride they now take in their work. Everyone feels the thrill of being an integral part of a growing company. Selecto-Flash is a renewed company with a tremendous future ahead.

—Valerie Shondel, CEO, Selecto-Flash, Inc., West Orange, NJ, www.selectoflash.com

Personnel

Everyone on your team has expectations, strengths, hopes, and fears. These play out in positive and negative ways. By acknowledging, affirming, and developing those on your team, you not only aid them, but you strengthen the whole. Just as we tend to take our long-term personal relationships for granted, we often begin to take those in work relationships for granted, too. We define them by what they do or don't do to keep the business thriving—or chugging along.

One way to infuse energy into your team is to look at your employees as though meeting them for the first time. You might start by reviewing resumes. What untapped skills and knowledge lurk there? How can you redirect your team members' strengths?

Review job descriptions, responsibilities, skills, and abilities. Many employees have strengths that they themselves might not view as assets. Notice how team members interact, step up to challenges, bring the extra effort or creative touch to a seemingly routine task. You may find cues and clues to hidden skills and talents that, if developed and/or acknowledged, would increase an employee's self-confidence, job performance, and value to your company.

Maybe the young woman you hired as an office assistant two years ago has developed substantial proofreading and customer service skills. Where do you need her talents? Which of them is most important to your business now? Think about how a promotion will affect the structure of your business. What will you lose by not taking action—possibly a valuable employee, frustrated about being underutilized?

Review Team Dynamics

Do employees feel stifled? Is one person's ego keeping another from contributing to the fullest? Is there conflict among the ranks? Continue to take stock, periodically, regarding how well your team is functioning as a team. If conflict has become a way of life for team members, if tempers flare, if anyone is afraid to speak up, don't ignore the situation. If you cannot resolve the problem or lay the groundwork for team members to solve it themselves, you may need to call in an expert to sort out the troubling dynamic.

QUICK Tip

Resolve style impasses: "We are all afraid of John. He throws things, yells, swears, and visibly shakes from anger when he is upset."

As a human resources consultant and facilitator, I am constantly amazed at how often a team culture can get trapped in what I call the cloud of the unknown, a place where we are confronted with obstacles that are resistant to rational problem-solving methods. It is a scary place for most people—filled with anger, bitterness, and rancor. In order to get to the heart of this thundercloud, we need to focus on the players—and not as cogs in the company wheel, but as unique individuals with complex and clashing human psyches. As I listened to each perspective, the reason for the problems began to clearly focus around two players: John and Mike.

A department manager for twenty years, upper management categorized John as loyal, dependable, efficient, and committed to a quality job. He confessed to feeling stifled in his current position with the organization. He had, in fact, applied for transfers out of his department with no luck. His boss was reticent to let him go because he was so dependable.

Mike, on the other hand, had twenty-five years with the organization and had performed nearly every position in the labor force. Recognized as being very fair and knowledgeable, he was committed to doing a good job and being a responsible supervisor to his staff. According to Mike, he had only one problem—John.

As I reviewed the team and clearly saw everyone's place in the organization, it became obvious that these personality clashes were not superficial. In fact, each party was firmly placed in his camp. It was clear that Mike and John didn't speak the same language. For example, Mike might approach John and say, "I'm trying to get my group to go to a job on time, so as an incentive, I'll buy them coffee if they're in ten minutes early." John would tirade, "That's ridiculous. If they are in a minute over time we'll dock their pay."

While many team members identified John as "the problem," it was Mike whose psychic shift changed the team culture. Mike was the opinion leader in the ranks; the other supervisors and staff took their lead from him. Although he was respected for his fairness and knowledge within the organization, he had long ago relinquished his power to John and stuffed his strengths in the closet. Mike had been fueling other team members' discontent while he proclaimed that he didn't need to change because John was the problem.

I used two personality profiles to show all team members, but especially Mike and John, the styles behind their clashes. Differences are fine as long as each respects the others, and everyone communicates clearly to move through conflict.

John began to accept the styles, communication, and problem-solving methods of others, allowing Mike to voice concerns and opinions. Mike was able to institute change by opening up to John as an individual with strengths and weakness rather than viewing him as a threat. The overall stress in the workplace diminished because of Mike's and John's newfound ability to collaborate.

The team now holds a monthly communications session to sort out what is working and what is not. The fact that they can now talk to each other is a key factor in their hopes for a more relaxed work environment and future successful professional collaboration.

—Adapted from "Tackling Organizational Conflict: Can This Team Be Saved?" (*Bulletin for Psychological Type*, Summer 2004) by Teresa Weed Newman (ENFP), Organizational Consultant for Project Innovations, Inc., Farmington Hills, MI

The Part-Time Employee Challenge

As you take stock of your team and your role in bringing out the best in each team member, don't overlook your part-time staff. Do your part-timers feel like part of the team? Some businesses rely primarily on competent, part-time help. Other businesses are staffed by full-time employees but bring in part-time help for specific needs or to round out their staff. Good part-time help is difficult to retain. Instilling loyalty in those who do not believe that they are an integral part of your team is a challenge.

Community and stability are often absent from the part-time worker's environment. They may suffer from what we call "the nomad syndrome" as they bounce from available place to available place with nowhere to hang their proverbial hats. Consequently, they may feel and be treated like intruders. They are important to your team and must know that. Emphasize to them and to others that the part-timers belong. Find a space—no matter how small—that is theirs. Depending upon your business and their roles, the space could be anything from a desk drawer or locker to a small desk, a computer station, or a corner in a conference room. Think of little things that matter to your full-time staffers and extend them to part-timers.

Ensure that part-timers know the big picture and are included in discussions that explain or affect their work. You may not be able to schedule staff meetings around fluid schedules; however, you can use some form of summary communication—hardcopy, email, bulletin board (electronic or not), or a five minute stand-up meeting to ensure that they are in the loop.

Leadership Activity: Know Your Team

This activity is best implemented in a trusting environment. Employees will not share the necessary information if they expect negative repercussions.

Distribute the following form to everyone on your internal team. Emphasize that honesty will help you realign human resources. Have each individual complete the form privately and then schedule individual discussions. Expect surprises.

Job Assessment
List your responsibilities below. Rate each one on a scale of 1–5.

Boring..... Stimulating
1   2   3   4   5

Key Responsibilities:

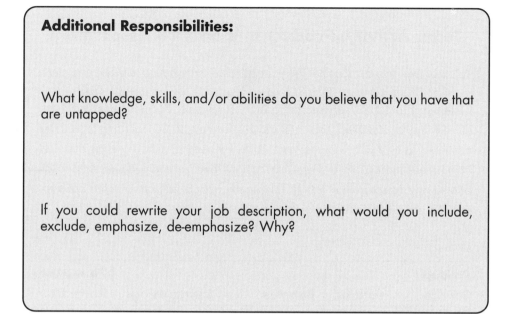

Additional Responsibilities:

What knowledge, skills, and/or abilities do you believe that you have that are untapped?

If you could rewrite your job description, what would you include, exclude, emphasize, de-emphasize? Why?

Product/Service Assessment

Define your products/services. Do they still meet the need they were intended to meet? What make your products/services more marketable than your competitors'? If nothing does, think about how you can change that. What features should you upgrade? What lines are no longer profitable? What are your competitors doing that you're not? Have you missed opportunities to grow in positive, new directions? Remember, it's never too late to get into the race. The pioneers got the kinks out for you. Have you gradually moved in too many directions? Now is the time to focus and reassess.

Think about a new product or service you might offer. What will make that successful? Think about positioning your newest addition and, perhaps, repositioning the tried and true. What's your edge? Why would a client or customer select your product or service over a competitor's?

Involve your team in this process. What can you learn from employees? Those with their ears to the ground can hear it rumble. Think of those to whom you've delegated key responsibilities and those in your front line. They know firsthand the threats and opportunities your company faces in a changing environment.

Team Activity: Product and Service Assessment

Ask your team to work together to fill out the following product/service assessment.

Note which products/services bring in most revenue. Focus on keeping these current and/or improved. Look at the lowest earners, those that bring in the least revenue. Do they pull resources that would be better spent on greater earners? Now check the middle earners. How might they be improved or enhanced? Should any be scrapped? Why? This simple activity can become the basis for revising your vision and realigning your goals.

Example:

Product/Service	Features	Benefits	Shortcomings	Percent of Revenue
Jewelry to hold eyeglasses	Unique, unisex, multilength chains	Glasses available when you need them; conversation piece; can be worn without glasses	Chains too weak; need to upgrade quality	5 percent (newest product)

Product/Service	Features	Benefits	Shortcomings	Percent of Revenue

QUICK Tip

Look in from the outside: Is your image (print/online) a strength or a weakness? Review your material, doing your best to see yourself as others would see you. Compare to competitors. What gets your attention? Whom would you choose to work with?

Your Stakeholders

As you begin to take stock, take a step back and answer this question: Who is on your team? You probably answered those who work in your business, either with or for you. Think bigger. Your team is more expansive than that. Although those in your business are important stakeholders, they are far from the only ones. A stakeholder is anyone affected by your business's output. They are all part of your team. Think about the scope of the resources you now have!

Clients, customers, financial backers, employees, suppliers, stockholders (should you be fortunate enough to have them), even family are stakeholders. They all have a stake in your business's success. Your suppliers, for instance, rely upon you for their success. In this reciprocal relationship, you are part of their team, as well. Your customers are stakeholders, too. They want quality service and products, reasonable prices, safety assurances, and the respect and service that every customer deserves.

The Importance of Stakeholders

Why are stakeholders important? They are your larger team. Knowing their expectations gives you additional information as your business grows. Can you meet every expectation of every stakeholder? That's doubtful. Often, stakeholder needs may be in conflict. Your bank wants you to tighten spending, your employees want raises, your suppliers raised their prices, and your customers want product/service improvements without cost increases. A sturdy foundation for goal setting and problem-solving will help you reach a rational compromise that keeps all your stakeholders content.

Are you aware of how your major stakeholders view performance and evaluate success? Stakeholders judge the worth of an organization according to how well it performs against the criteria of the stakeholders—not the organization's criteria.

Use the exercise below to identify your specific stakeholders, their expectations of you and your business, and your assessment of how you meet those expectations.

Leadership Activity: Stakeholder Identification and Analysis

Identify your stakeholders, using the following steps:

1. Identify the stakeholders and their stake in the organization. Have others in your organization help you brainstorm a list of stakeholders. Don't prioritize; just write. Think about those your business touches and those who touch your business.

2. Determine, in general, how much influence various stakeholders should have.

3. Use the "Stakeholder Analysis Worksheet" for yourself, then give it to your team to use as a teambuilding activity that will give you additional perspective.

Now, use the "Stakeholder Analysis Worksheet" below to: (1) list major stakeholders, (2) identify major stakeholder criteria, and (3) assess how well your organization performs in light of those criteria.

Be sure to include your most important stakeholder group: your clients or customers. Depending on the size of your team, have team members work individually, with partners, or in small groups. Have each individual or subteam use the analysis for a particular stakeholder. You may have requested this activity from a number of departments; the confluence and divergence of answers will be interesting jumping-off points for strengthening your team.

Example:

Stakeholder Analysis Worksheet

Stakeholder

First Bank

Criteria Used By Stakeholder to Assess Our Performance

Regular payments to reduce line of credit (LOC)

Cash balance in line with checks written on account

Self-Assessment of Our Performance

On target

Stakeholder Analysis Worksheet

Stakeholder

Criteria Used By Stakeholder to Assess Our Performance

Self-Assessment of Our Performance (According to These Criteria)

Are stakeholder expectations realistic? Is your business falling short of the mark? Review you vision and your goals. Meet with your primary team to determine whether or not changes are in order. Often, the outsider's perspective can show you a picture of your company and its performance that you and your team have overlooked. Don't discount the seemingly irrelevant recommendation.

Take Care of Your Team

Everyone comes to work with baggage—some heavier than others. Family-friendly work policies and an empathic workplace make personal challenges easier to handle and allow people to focus on the tasks at hand.

Companies large and small are adapting to keep pace with the recognition of the importance of balance. Not only does the balanced approach help employees address issues of child-care, prolonged illness, aging parents, and more, but it offers the employer an employee who has the peace of mind to focus when at work. Balance creates a productive team.

Employee input and commitment should also be taken into account when considering whether a necessary policy might bend. In times of family crises, people are distracted enough without worrying about unyielding policies and losing their jobs should they do what is necessary to take care of business at home.

QUICK Tip

Keeping a balance: Lurita Doan, former president and CEO of New Technology Management, Inc. (NTM) with corporate offices in Reston, Virginia, recognized the value of flexibility. To help meet her employees' needs, Lurita rolled her company's sixteen personal days (ten vacation, five sick days, and one birthday) into an employee-friendly package that "can be cashed in at any time, accrued, or rolled over from year to year" thus allowing long vacations or lengthy visits to overseas homelands. Doan put many provisions in place to ensure a happy and healthy workforce, including providing employees with "an exciting and stimulating work environment that presents employees with sustained intellectual challenge" and "opportunities for professional growth and upward mobility within the company."

Doan sold NTMI in 2005 and has been nominated by President Bush to be the administrator of the General Services Administration with 15,000 employees in 2,700 federal buildings and the largest technology acquisition portfolio of all of the federal government agencies.

Remember the importance of acknowledgment, rewards, and perks: As discussed, creating an environment of acknowledgment and praise will make for a happier and more productive team. Acknowledge employees publicly. Share the limelight when you receive an award. You know you didn't earn it alone. No one does. Take a step back and shine the light on others in your organization. Recommend them for honors, awards, prestigious committees, or assignments. Everyone appreciates being appreciated. Creative options to demonstrate their value to you and your appreciation of them abound. The company that works to acknowledge its employees takes another step toward building a cohesive, motivated team.

Many of us (not all) relish our special days: birthdays, employment anniversaries, and the Hallmark holidays (from Valentine's Day to Administrative Assistant Day). Read your team to determine the appropriate action and celebrate in a way that works for you, your budget, and your team. Even a simple birthday card will make an employee feel noticed and appreciated.

Then, of course, there are the more tangible honors: certificates, plaques, and trophies. These are appropriate for outstanding achievements and, sometimes, for being the wind beneath someone else's wings or being part of a synergistic, high-producing team.

And don't forget the value of money: bonuses, stock options, and merit increases may not tug at anyone's heartstrings, but all of these demonstrate a company's willingness to invest in its employees.

Some creative options for rewarding employees include implementing a point system that allows employees to build up points for gifts ranging from retail gift certificates to cruises (depending on your rewards budget). These catalog options allow team members to choose their own rewards and, potentially, choose between smaller rewards more often or saving up for a more substantial one. Customization of rewards is always a perk when it comes to motivation.

As you take stock, review your policies and processes to identify those that enhance and those that detract from creating that critical balance.

Chapter  10

Expanding Your Internal Team

"A championship team is a team of champions." —Unknown

▶ **Expansion: Risk vs. Reward**

▶ **Hiring**

▶ **The Interview**

▶ **Culture Patterns**

Expansion: Risk vs. Reward

Expansion comes with a myriad of options. Sometimes, the first step toward expansion is the recognition that you, alone, cannot be the business. Then come the time-consuming tasks of identifying the correct vehicle for expansion, the right time, and the necessary resources. For many businesses, growth requires bringing in more full- or part-time employees.

The entrepreneur often walks the fine line between being risk phobic and overly optimistic. For example, you have your own accounting firm and hired slowly and wisely to keep pace with steady growth. Your clients, for the most part, have been in the small-to-mid-size range. During the past several years, you have moved to more of a management and consulting role, working with fewer clients and managing your growing business and expanding team. You are now approached by the CFO of a multimillion-dollar business. This will change your structure and affect your existing team. Questions to ponder:

- Are you the only one in your firm qualified to meet this client's needs? If so, you need to reassess your current team.
- Is someone on your team capable of working with you and getting to your level of skill and knowledge quickly (whatever quickly may be)?
- Do you need to hire another accountant at your level of expertise?
- Do you approach a colleague to form a strategic alliance with you to free you to spend most of your time with the new client?
- Or do you pass up the brass ring?

Sometimes, a seemingly great opportunity comes at a time when following through might not be in the business's best interest. Always weigh risks and rewards. Sometimes the greatest reward is realizing that the track you're on is going in the right direction.

The Effects on the Team

Beyond bringing new people into your organization, expansion means helping existing staff accept the changing dynamic and the direct effects on them. As people work in specific roles and assume responsibilities, they also assume ownership of those roles and responsibilities. Some extend that sense of ownership to processes and the work product. Certainly, you've noticed how many people, some to a greater extent than others, don't want anyone "messing with," "interfering with," "screwing up" their "stuff." While this may be a legitimate concern at times, often the need for someone to jump in isn't always anticipated and cannot be avoided.

Apply the ownership principal to the small office. The "everything support person," who has been the backbone of the organization for years, now must hand over some responsibility to someone new. Granted, this person has carried too great a burden for too long. Work has slipped through the cracks because of the overload. This mainstay of your organization has, during recent months, complained about having only two hands and two ears. Does that mean that she's ready to welcome an opportunity to delegate or to share responsibility with open arms? Doubtful.

QUICK Tip

Explore your hiring options: Hiring is a strategic action that you want to fit into an overall business plan. Examine your vision and goals. How does your current staff help you work toward them? Would training or retraining be more cost effective? Would reallocation of resources, moving people from one responsibility to another, or increasing responsibility solve your problem? Or is hiring the best solution?

Hiring

Bringing people into your organization is a critical step that requires a combination of skill and intuition. By hiring, you are inviting people to participate in your dream.

Find the best person for the job. Finding a person you like and trying to fit that person into the job is usually a bad idea. At times, however, employers (especially small business owners) "happen upon" the right fit. Don't discount someone just because the time, the background, or person may seem a little off the mark, but this is not an endorsement of hiring every "not quite right, but I really like her" person who crosses your path. The first step in finding the right person for the job is having a clear idea of what the job is and the skills and abilities necessary to succeed at it.

Most entrepreneurs recognize that their time is better spent on the "business of the business"—concentrating on the big-picture responsibilities that will cause growth and bring in capital. They begin by hiring support staff to handle calls, scheduling, or keep order in the office—these are no small feats, especially considering that positions in start-up organizations usually involve responsibilities the business owner hadn't thought of in hiring. The relationship built by start-up entrepreneurs and early support staff often create long-lasting bonds and a support system that is not only helpful on-the-job, but personally enriching.

Soon, however, you will need that next level. Consider who will be able to wear one of those hats that you're so reluctant to relinquish: sales, marketing, research, writing, financial management, and so much more. Now you face the daunting task of letting go. You will never find a clone, but you can find qualified people with their own styles and much to add.

QUICK Tip

Use instinct as well as protocol: Our small training and development business, Diamond Associates (NJ), needed additional support staff. After placing an ad in the local paper, our office manager used phone interviews to narrow the field of candidates qualified for the face-to-face interview. We needed someone with solid computer skills, good English—both written and spoken, and the ability to work in a hectic environment with shifting priorities.

The office manager screened well, and we had a number of candidates qualified for the position. She then told us of a woman she had spoken with who had responded to our ad: She had a PhD in French, recently taught Italian, and was currently working as a receptionist in a yoga studio. No match here. But she sounded so interesting. Why not meet her? Meet her we did, scrapping our trusty interview guide and just talking. Nancy was so engaging, so much a team player, so eager and talented, we could not discount her. We hired someone else for the clerical position, but suggested that Nancy join the firm as an intern, helping with a variety of tasks as needed and we would determine a fit. She worked on program design and development, client meetings and phone calls, trainer coordination, clerical tasks, and more. Quickly, we realized her value and promoted her to director of client relations. Had we followed all the rules, Nancy never would have entered the door. What a loss that would have been!

Is a Job Description Really Necessary?

Yes! Creating a complete, detailed job description will help you in your search, then help your new hire understand the full scope of your expectations. Some areas may be flexible; that's fine. You are even allowed to change your requirements, but if you don't start with something solid, your search will be too scattered. Whether you are using a placement service that will be using the job description as a guideline for finding the right person or just using it to clarify the position for yourself as you embark on your search, a job description is essential.

Figure 10.1: **WRITING JOB DESCRIPTIONS**

1. Clearly define the job requirements.

2. List the key responsibility areas.

3. Identify and rank the knowledge, skills, and abilities (KSAs) that are needed to perform the job.

4. Identify the key actions for success: What does it take to do the job well?

Alert!

Create a candidate pool: Traditionally, companies get serious about hiring when they have a specific opening: "Our vice president of marketing quit, so we need a new one," or "We want to enter the market for a new kind of computer chip, so we need a team of designers." I call that approach "coincidence hiring." "I happen to need a basketball player today. Did Michael Jordan happen to quit his job?" The odds that he did are not very good. So what are the odds of your landing him?

—Source: "How to Hire the Next Michael Jordan," by Gina Imperato, from an interview with John Sullivan (the "Michael Jordan of Hiring"), *Fast Company* magazine

Build Your Database

Wouldn't hiring be a breeze if you already had prequalified, fully competent candidates lined up before a position opened? You can, and many business owners, managers, and team builders do. Build your database of viable candidates before you have the need to hire. Those you identify may not be looking, and you may not have a position open when you encounter or learn about someone you would like to have on your team. Keep names and contact information (with notes) in a special database of talented people. You might send email updates to stay in touch. If one of those prospective candidates decides to leave his or her present position, you want to be foremost on the job search list.

If you have a small job to offer that does not require a potential hire leaving his or her present employment, this gives both you and the hire the advantage of "trying on" the relationship. By building relationships, you create interest and a path for new talent to eventually join your team. Just as headhunters advise employees to always be looking for the next opportunity, so must employers always be on the lookout as well.

Search Options

"Good help is hard to find" has always been the employer's lament, but "good help"—from experienced professionals to bright, motivated novices—is out there. Where do you find that perfect match for the position? Think outside the classified ad box and consider using a number of resources. Some have fees associated; others do not. Some of the more costly options may be well worth the price, depending on the value of the position you need filled. Consider all options; use more than one. A capable team is the foundation of your business's growth.

• Internet Job Search Sites

Job sites allow you to post ads, search resumes, and even organize potential candidates. Search by keyword or such distinctions as most recent employer, most recent job description, schools attended, desired salary, location. You can choose level of experience, full time, part time, or per diem, and further limit your results to those seeking employment, internship, temporary contract work, and seasonal work. Your search will bring up full resumes and contact information. Employers pay a fee on most sites, but consider the benefits.

• Newspaper Want Ads

Newspaper want ads never go out of style and most now have the added dimension of being displayed online. Newspapers also reach people online sources may not.

• Internal Postings

Consider hiring from within. If your company is large enough to have multiple departments, internal postings can offer welcomed opportunities for change. Even for a small business with a handful of employees, reorganizing responsibilities can energize your team. See chapter 10: "Expanding Your Internal Team" for more about internal talent.

• Professional Recruiters

Working with a search firm that understands your needs can speed up the process and save you or your employees a lot of legwork, right down to the nitty-gritty of checking references (and, yes, references should be checked).

• Employment Agencies

Again, the process costs money but saves legwork, and a good firm will access talent. Success depends upon your clearly stating your needs and feeling confident that the agency understands them. If it seems as though an agency is taking shots in the dark, move on. You don't have time to waste with unqualified candidates. If you have concerns about the right fit, find one that specializes in your field and has a solid track record.

• Temp Agencies

Hiring temporary help is a good opportunity to evaluate the fit and skills of a potential full-time hire. Hire a support person to help out or fill in for a week or two, or hire a professional to work on a specific project before offering full time.

• **Networking**
Networking extends to everyone you know. The more people who know that you are looking for employees, the more people are on the lookout for you. You have an ad hoc search team. Don't, however, promise your neighbor that you have a job for his cousin. Add her to your candidate pool.

• **Job Fairs**
You can get a table or just walk around. By having a table, you attract job seekers interested in your type of business and have a chance to share print and verbal information, collect names and addresses, even have a short pre-application available. Without a table, you can still network and exchange cards or information. See who is showing an interest in your field and approach them.

• **The Retiree Pool**
Those who retire or are sent off with fanfare and golden parachutes to make way for a new generation after decades-long careers have impressive backgrounds and skills and are often eager to contribute to a growing company of any size. They may fit into your part-time, subcontractor, or full-time pool. One source for locating these workers is the "Resources for Employers" section at www.aarp.org.

• **College Placement Offices**
Reaching out to schools is a way to find qualified people who are just starting out, which often creates a win/win situation with small business owners. The recent college graduate may not bring a wealth of experience but does bring skills, knowledge, enthusiasm, and an eagerness to learn from you and about your business. The college student that you hire can also serve as a great resource for additional or future help.
College placement offices won't easily find you if you're a small business. Through partnering with a local college or university, you can tap into a department that will work with you and provide students studying your field and eager for on-the-job experience. The college intern brings a fresh perspective and spirited motivation.

• **High Schools**

If you're looking for part-time, no-experience-necessary employees, consider reaching out to the local high school. Often, high school students bring technical skills and a willingness to do what needs to be done. They do need clear direction and an understanding of your organization's work ethic.

• **Local Job Training Programs**

Before (or during) searching through cyberspace, consider checking local job training programs for qualified candidates. For a variety of reasons, good workers with strong skills end up in these funded programs. Additionally, people who have little or no employment experience complete job training programs eager to become productive. These programs also assist people who have been out of the work force in returning to it. They may have previous, relevant experience.

• **Overseas Options**

We all know that often when we reach customer phone support staff, we are speaking long distance; many products are manufactured overseas. A good share of U.S. company computer graphics, web designs, and online program developments are also produced overseas.

Identify KSAs

In addition to key responsibility areas, every job requires certain knowledge, skills, and abilities (KSAs). Prior to the interview, you must establish these requirements and the actions that demonstrate them. This information not only ensures that you ask the right questions during the interview, but also creates criteria to help you differentiate among candidates during the selection phase.

For example:

KSA: Teamwork

Definition: Working effectively with a team or others within or outside the formal reporting relationship to accomplish goals, taking actions that respect the opinions and contributions of others, facilitating and accepting consensus, working toward team goals that either encompass or override personal objectives.

Key Actions:
- Build relationships.
- Exchange information freely.
- Volunteer ideas.
- Build on others' ideas.
- Support group decisions and processes.
- Put group goals first.

KSA: Problem Solving

Definition: Working to develop alternative strategies to resolve a problem or issue through reviewing logical assumptions, creative options, and information. Take into consideration resources (personnel and financial), constraints, and organizational values in order to arrive at the most satisfactory solution.

Key Actions:
- Define decision criteria.
- Consider alternatives.
- Consider all relevant facts.
- Balance pros, cons, and impact of alternatives.
- Communicate with, request input from, and inform others as appropriate.
- Commit to the most appropriate action.

Leadership Activity: KSAs

Identify several KSAs needed for a position in your company. For each one, complete the template. Include ranking the KSAs importance to the job on a scale of 1 (minimal) to 5 (essential).

KSA: Rank:

Definition:

Key Actions:

•

•

-
-
-

KSA: Rank:
Definition:

Key Actions:

-

-

-

-

-

KSA: Rank:
Definition:

Key Actions:

-

-

-

-

-

Now, apply this process to a current or potential opening within your company.

The Interview

Many view interviewing as a tedious process. Sometimes, when interviewing numerous people within a short time period, faces, names, and credentials tend to run together. The behavioral interview questions introduced in this section should allow you draw out information about candidates' past actions (and reactions) in specific work-related situations and hear their current assessments of their own behavior. This process will help you decide among candidates using a consistent protocol for all. You will gain insights not only into their knowledge, skills, and abilities, but their reactions to a variety of situations and their approaches to problem solving.

Figure 10.2: PREPARATION CHECKLIST AND REMINDERS

Preparation Checklist and Reminders

- Review the application materials, including resume.
- Decide which of their jobs/experiences are most relevant to the job.
- Prepare and review your core list of behavioral questions.
- Prepare questions to review the candidate's background—consider any jobs/experiences about which you are uncertain or would like additional information. Note any gaps in employment or any other anomaly you may wish to review with the candidate.
- Review the KSAs and the key actions.

Remember:

- Try to talk less than 25 percent of the time.
- Take good notes.
- Be aware of your own biases and prejudices. Don't let them get in the way of your listening or your decision-making process.
- Do not be influenced by the first one in or the last one out.
- Consider personal attributes that would inhibit job success: a lack of flexibility, a dislike of working alone or on a team.

Plan your interview carefully. Develop an interview guide based on KSAs to ensure consistency. Planning helps you focus, elicit the right information, spend the appropriate amount of time, and give all candidates the attention that they deserve. Take time to review resumes. The quick scan-as-you-sit-down-with-the-interviewee approach may miss key points. You may not see an opportunity to probe for more information about experience or skills.

The Interview Format

Your interview should follow a logical format. Key areas will be your introduction, review of candidate's experience, questions, and closing.

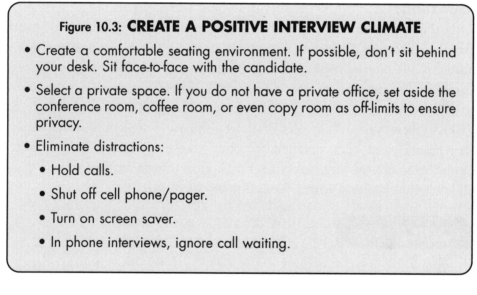

Figure 10.3: CREATE A POSITIVE INTERVIEW CLIMATE

- Create a comfortable seating environment. If possible, don't sit behind your desk. Sit face-to-face with the candidate.

- Select a private space. If you do not have a private office, set aside the conference room, coffee room, or even copy room as off-limits to ensure privacy.

- Eliminate distractions:
  - Hold calls.
  - Shut off cell phone/pager.
  - Turn on screen saver.
  - In phone interviews, ignore call waiting.

Introduction

In your introduction, your goals should be to develop rapport, set expectations as to process and interview protocol, and put the candidate at ease. Only a comfortable candidate will be able to provide the level of information that best indicates future performance.

1. Greet the candidate, giving your name and position.
2. Explain the purpose and time frame of the interview. (Generally, the purpose is for the employer and candidate to learn about each other and gauge "fit.")

3. Explain the interview structure.

Sample structure:

- Brief job overview
- Information about the position and the organization
- Brief review of candidate's experience
- Specific questions to get specific information about their experience
- Opportunity for questions

4. Mention note taking. Point out that you may take notes to ensure that you remember pertinent information. Mentioning it up front will ease possible discomfort or distraction.

Questions

Questions serve to review previous experience and get a feel for style and possible future performance. Questions come in many forms, some more useful to the interview process than others. Remember the open and closed questions discussed in chapter 4 (page 82). When the interviewer requires a straightforward, concise response from the candidate, closed questions (which elicit "yes/no" answers or short responses) are appropriate. Open questions (which elicit detailed responses) are best when your goal is to probe for understanding, clarify, seek additional information, or assess a candidate's comfort level with a particular topic.

QUICK Tip

Seven Basic Interview Questions

1. What do you like most/least about your most recent position?

2. Why are you looking to leave your current job?

3. What special skills do you have that suit you for this position?

4. Describe a recent situation during which you had to use those skills.

5. What was the most satisfying aspect of your most recent employment?

6. What do you know about our company and its corporate structure?

7. What major trends do you foresee for our industry in the next three to five years?

Ask the Right Questions

Overall, open questions are most effective in the interview process. Changing your style from closed to open questions may not be easy. Practice opening closed questions. Rather than, "Do you enjoy challenging work?" Ask, "What do you enjoy about challenging work?" Hypothetical and behavioral questions both fall into the category of open questions, each encouraging the prospective team member to provide more information.

Hypothetical questions are based on "what if" scenarios. Some interviewers use them to predict future on-the-job behaviors. These are fine, but remember: hypothetical questions yield hypothetical answers. Most candidates will answer these questions with "best case" scenario responses. They will say what they anticipate that you want to hear. Even if they answer in earnest with what they believe (or at least wish) they would do, those questions may not be the best indicator of future performance.

What would you do if _____?

How would you respond to ____?

Behavioral questions are the most useful interview questions. These concrete questions about how someone has acted in the past typically offer a realistic vision of possible future actions. Although not foolproof, they do give you a good idea of how a candidate behaves, reacts, and thinks. They call upon something that actually happened rather than just a hypothetical situation.

- Tell me about a time when…?
- What did you do in that situation?
- What did you say?

These questions will help drive the discussion to reveal strengths as well as potential problem areas. You don't have to stick strictly to the script. Behavioral questions also create openings for natural follow-up questions that will keep the discussion and information naturally flowing.

Closed Question: Are you good at motivating people?

Possible Answer: "Absolutely!"

Simple Open Question: What do you do to motivate people?

Possible Answer: "I'm very supportive and encouraging."

Hypothetical Question: Suppose you were on a team on which one member consistently neglected to speak up in meetings. What would you do to motivate this person's participation?

Possible Answer: "I would talk with that person privately and stress that I know that he/she has a lot to offer and that the team would benefit from his or her input."

Behavioral Question: Describe a situation in which you motivated employees or coworkers.

Possible Answer: "We had to work overtime to meet a very tightly imposed, last-minute deadline. The client was in a bind, and, consequently, so were we. I explained the importance of this client and the reason for the unreasonable deadline. I told my staff that I knew that they could come through although the timing was difficult. I brought in dinner for those who could stay and offered a reasonable comp time arrangement for everyone."

Leadership Activity

To get a feel for the varied responses elicited by these question types, think about ways that an interviewee might reply to the questions below:

Closed: "Are you comfortable with change?"
Open: "How do you manage change?"
Hypothetical: "How would you react if you were told the company was relocating out of state?"
Behavioral: "Tell me about a time that you were faced with a major change at work and what you did to manage it."

Closed: "Do you handle stress well?"
Open: "Tell me how you handle stress."
Hypothetical: "How would you manage a downsizing transition to minimize employee stress?"
Behavioral: "How are you handling the stress of downsizing in your current management role?"

Figure 10.4: **BEHAVIORAL ASSESSMENT QUESTIONS**

Below is a list of behavioral questions designed to help you assess the candidate's level of proficiency for specific, critical team skills.

Communication:

1. Describe a misunderstanding you had with a coworker or supervisor. What steps did you take to straighten things out?

2. Tell me about a time when you communicated a message to someone who didn't want to hear it. How did you know? What did you say?

Conflict Resolution:

3. Describe a time when someone was angry with you at work. How did you handle the situation?

4. Think of a time when you and someone you had to work with just didn't "click." What special efforts did you take to make the relationship work? What were the results?

Planning and Organizing:

5. Describe the steps you take to plan and organize your day effectively.

6. Describe a situation at work that required several things to be done at the same time. What did you do?

7. We have all had times when we just couldn't get everything done on time. Tell me about a time when this has happened to you. What did you do?

Detail Orientation:

8. Describe a time when you had to focus on the "big picture" without losing attention to detail. What challenges did you face? What steps did you take to ensure that details were attended to?

9. Can you think of a project or task that you work on that required attention to detail? What did you do to ensure that all bases were covered?

Teamwork/Collaboration:

10. Interacting with others can be challenging at times. Tell me about a specific time when you had difficulty getting along with peers, team members, or others at work. How did you handle the situation?

11. When dealing with team members (or a group), it's difficult to know when you are being overly demanding. Tell me about a time when you may have been overly demanding.

12. Tell me about the last idea you shared with a peer/team member.

13. Describe the most challenging (frustrating, difficult) work experience you've had and how you handled it.

Negotiation:

14. Describe your most satisfying/disappointing experience in negotiating a disagreement on policy or procedure with senior management.

15. What types of negotiating techniques have you used? Describe a situation in which you used them.

16. Can you think of a time when you had to arrive at a compromise or guide others to one? How did you handle that?

Adaptability:

17. Tell me about a time when a business situation took an unexpected turn. What did you think? What did you do?

18. Can you remember a situation in which you had to adapt your strategy to align with the customer needs or organizational strategy? What did you do?

19. Describe the last major change that caused disruption in a work situation. How did you handle it? What did you do to adapt and move forward?

20. What major trends do you foresee for our industry? What plans do you have to be ready for those changes?

Legal Questions

The interview process must follow careful legal guidelines. Chances are, you don't have a legal department to guide you, as large corporations do. That doesn't mean that you are not accountable for following the correct protocol. The legality of a question may change over time, so be certain to check for the most recent guidelines or speak to your lawyer about any questions that may be—well—questionable.

In most cases, it is not legal to ask questions regarding age, sex, marital status, race, religion, disability, veteran classification, or national origin. Discriminating based on any of the above is illegal.

Leadership Activity: Legal Question Quiz

We designed this quiz to raise your awareness of questions that fall into the "okay to ask" and "don't ask" category. Labor laws, their interpretation, and their nuances change. Review any suspect questions, even those in our quiz, with your attorney.

Are the following questions legal? Write "Y" for yes and "N" for no.

Y/N

1. When did you graduate from college?

2. Where did you get that charming accent?

3. Where were you born?

4. What is your religion?

5. What is your maiden name?

6. Who will take care of your children while you are working?

7. How have you managed child-care in the past?

8. What is your title—Ms. or Mrs.?

9. How does your husband/wife feel about these late hours?

10. Have you ever worked under another name?

11. Submit proof of age (birth certificate or baptismal record).

12. Are you available for Saturday or Sunday work?

13. Are you a citizen of the U.S.?

14. Are you a naturalized citizen?

15. Do you have appropriate documentation to work in the U.S.?

16. Have you ever used illegal drugs?

17. List social organizations, clubs, societies, and lodges to which you belong.

18. Networking is an important part of this job. What, if any, professional organizations do you currently belong to?

19. Will you need time off at Passover?

20. What foreign languages can you read, write, or speak?

21. Have you ever been arrested for any crime? If so, when and where?

22. Have you ever been convicted of a crime?

23. Have you ever had your wages garnished?

24. Do you own a home?

25. Attach a photograph to the application form.

26. May I see pictures of your children?

27. What kind of work does your spouse do?

28. This job requires heavy lifting and long hours on your feet. Will that be a problem for you?

29. Please list on the application any physical handicaps you have.

30. Do you currently use illegal drugs?

Answer Key Legal Question Quiz

1. No	11. No	21. No
2. No	12. Yes	22. Yes
3. No	13. No	23. No
4. No	14. No	24. No
5. No	15. Yes	25. No
6. No	16. No	26. No
7. No	17. No	27. No
8. No	18. Yes	28. Yes
9. No	19. No	29. No
10. Yes	20. Yes	30. Yes

Closing

Use a wrap-up question to show that the interview is reaching a conclusion. Ask, "Is there anything else you wanted to tell me about that I did not give you a chance to discuss?" "Do you have any additional questions?"

Even if you're sure "This is the one!" don't jump to conclusions or offers. Thank each candidate, and share your follow-up plan and time frame.

Figure 10.5: SELECTION

1. Using the criteria you established prior to the interview, rate the applicant on each of the KSAs.

2. Review the rankings you assigned to each criterion.

3. Compare candidates based on the ratings and rankings.

4. Consult your "gut instinct."

5. Check references.

Figure 10.6: POST-INTERVIEW REFERENCE SHEET

Candidate: _____

Memory Jogger: _____

Rank KSAs in order of importance, then rate on a scale of 1 to 5.

5—Significantly exceeds criteria for successful performance

4—Exceeds criteria for successful performance

3—Meets criteria

2—Less than acceptable

1—Significantly less than acceptable

	KSA	5	4	3	2	1
1.	—	—	—	—	—	—
2.	—	—	—	—	—	—
3.	—	—	—	—	—	—
4.	—	—	—	—	—	—
5.	—	—	—	—	—	—
6.	—	—	—	—	—	—
7.	—	—	—	—	—	—
8.	—	—	—	—	—	—

Other Comments:

Culture Patterns

Every company has a culture. Company cultures reflect those values that are a common thread throughout. These are evident in the company's vision and goals and in the concrete actions of the team. That culture encompasses everything from the ethical climate to the tradition of Friday morning donuts and coffee. Cultures often have a certain energy to them, as well. Many find they have created a culture that works well for the team but is hard to define.

Newcomers may change your dynamic; expect some resettling time. Not everyone will fit neatly into all established culture patterns, and there is something to be said for shaking things up a little and for individuals operating in their own unique ways. They may even have a new way of doing things that can spark enhancements or improvements. While new and different can be positive and invigorating, it can also be stressful for team members when the status quo is upset; encourage patience.

However, many aspects of your company's image are important for team members to adopt and convey to the outside world. The culture that you create is your business's identity, and you don't want to tamper with it lightly; you also want your employees to embody it. This identity is comprised of the larger patterns that cover your internal and external customer service absolutes, general office protocols, and your approach to issues that fall into gray "ethical" areas.

Does the new team member's style fit your company image and convey the proper message to your clients or customers? Many of us have had the experience of interviewing and selecting the person who had the knowledge and skills required, who seemed to be the perfect fit. Then, from day one (or maybe day two) on the job, the tension among all team members became palpable. No one anticipated the level of "handholding," "I'll do it my own way thank you," or "You really let them ask that of you?" that has suddenly flooded your environment.

Early screening and trial periods make it easy for you and your team to evaluate your choice without feeling locked in or overly committed to forcing a fit. As part of your intake and training process, watch to see how team members represent you and your business. Hold that evaluation as a standard for all new team members. If the new team member openly (or quietly) undermines or refuses to adhere to processes that keep your team running smoothly, if he or she doesn't buy in to your idea of a quality standard, give second chances and clear developmental feedback, but know when to accept that it's a bad fit and move on.

Team Activity: Creating the Best Fit

Enlisting your team in determining what you need and how to find the right "fit" is a practical team activity. Whether you are adding an integral position to the small office or expanding a work team in a larger environment, before you develop your interview guide, talk to the people who will work shoulder-to-shoulder with the new person. Follow the guidelines below to generate a discussion to define your work culture and the work styles/behaviors that will complement and enhance it, and keep the results on hand for the next time you're looking to hire.

Directions:

1. Share the job description with your team. Generate a brief discussion of the roles and responsibilities of the new hire.

2. Depending on the size of the team, ask individuals, partners, or small groups to define the team's goals and the team role that they envision for the new hire.

3. Generate a discussion of how the new hire would fit into the existing team. To whom would he/she report? With whom will he/she work most closely? Who will train him/her?

4. Ask each person, partnership, or group to brainstorm those characteristics and behaviors that propel the team to excellence. You want someone who will work well with this team. However, you don't want a cookie-cutter fit either. Strive to achieve a balance.

5. Stress that by hiring someone to join the team, you plan to strengthen it. You want the new person to be comfortable questioning the tried and true and offering suggestions. You don't want a rubber stamp person, and you anticipate that your team doesn't either. Explain your vision for the new hire's roles and responsibilities.

6. If you developed an Interview Guide for this position, share it with your team and ask for feedback and recommendations. Revise as needed. If you haven't drafted an interview guide, have the team develop one.

7. Test your Interview Guide in a mock interview.

Integrating the New Team Member

If everyone starts on a team together, bonding takes place over time. Adding a new person to an existing team changes the group dynamic. This change is inevitable.

Do what you can to create a space where all new team members feel part of the group, and the group can appreciate new talent without feeling threatened. You can ease tension and smooth the transition by following some guidelines:

- When hiring, submit everyone to the same critique and standards. This creates cohesion in the team and also gives you a fair opportunity to monitor and guide someone who is new on your team.
- In a small company, your interview team might include others who will work closely with the new employee.
- Provide an introduction to the company both verbally and in writing that includes its vision and goals, its client base, and key culture patterns.
- Do what you can to ensure that all new team members feel part of the group and the group appreciates new members.

Chapter

Don't Grow It Alone

"Teamwork is the fuel that allows common people to attain uncommon results."
—Anonymous

▶ **Networking**

▶ **Advisory Boards**

▶ **Growth Strategies**

▶ **External Resources**

▶ **Remember the Home Team**

Networking

What can you learn from competitors and colleagues? If you have not yet joined industry, trade, or other business organizations, do it now. Yes, it takes time and may require eating more chicken than you're accustomed to, but the investment is worthwhile. Take advice from people who are where you want to be and give advice to those who are traveling on your well-worn path. By networking with colleagues, you open doors to information that is not always readily available. You learn about trends and plans that might affect your business's growth or health. You develop relationships with community leaders, colleagues, and competitors, all of whom know something that can give you an edge.

Join organizations and contribute time, but be careful not to overwhelm yourself and under-deliver. While you gain visibility and contacts through volunteer posts, you will only hurt your reputation by not following through on commitments. As with any investment, only put in what you can afford to do without. You will get a return on your investment, but never put in so much that your business suffers for it.

How to Meet People

Organizations focused on bringing together professionals abound and range from local to global, industry-focused, cross-industry, and mission-focused. Their goal can be networking, lead exchanges, advising, making barter connections, lobbying, or bringing organizations together for a larger purpose. Have you looked into your local or state chamber of commerce? If you haven't been making connections, talk to people and get online; find an organization that suits you and one to which your contributions will be valuable.

Don't join organizations anticipating an immediate payoff. Many business owners attend one or two networking events and then cross off that organization because "nothing happened" and move on to the next. Not surprisingly, none pays off for them. They missed the point of networking: developing relationships and building trust, both of which take time. The "networking butterfly" never alights long enough for either of these to grow.

Some networking groups, however, exist specifically for lead exchanges. These are small teams created by invitation who meet regularly to offer leads and referrals. No two members are in the same business; at some point everyone leaves with one or more solid leads.

> ### Figure 11.1: **THE SUCCESSFUL NETWORKER:**
> - Listens
> - Patiently develops relationships
> - Builds trust
> - Doesn't collar and sell

Online Networking

Reach out to related businesses to suggest linking to each other on the web. Consider networking through newsgroups. Do you know someone whose website features articles on your subject? If not, scroll around and submit. You may already know someone and have thought "I don't have time for that," but appearing as the expert with your contact information and site link is valuable free press. Do you go to trade shows? Why not look into virtual trade shows. The WYSIWYG (what you see is what you get) user format is usually very easy to follow and allows you to upload your business cards, articles, promotional material, bio (and team bio), and even record your voice welcoming visitors to your booth and introducing your business. Fill your booth with voice and video if you'd like. Visitors can "leave their business cards" at the booth and, by the end, you have a database of people who have seen your presentation and are interested in learning more.

Advisory Boards

An advisory board is a group of people selected to advise a business owner or organization. Board members are usually invited to join based on the knowledge, skills, and other assets they can bring to the table. Typically, advisory boards are comprised of people selected because of their abilities to give business owners advice on issues ranging from strategic planning, staffing, marketing, and other growth factors. Sometimes, however, they are made up of customers providing feedback for existing and potential products or services.

Often, while business owners welcome customer feedback, they shy away from more formal, involved business advisors for several reasons. Key among these are "I don't want anyone telling me what to do" and "I don't want to share my financial information." As you will see in the sections that follow, advisory boards don't tell or control, they advise. And when you are seeking detailed advice about growth and investment, unless your advisors know your financial situation—the good, the bad, and the ugly—they are working with their hands tied. Advisory boards, however you choose to create and engage them, enhance your power and bring additional experience to your decision-making process.

Peer Advisory Boards

Beyond networking organizations, look into peer advisory and support groups. Peer advisory boards can range from three or four people meeting in a restaurant or at someone's home or office to Internet forums meeting online or posting questions to invite members to add input in their own time. Of course, many levels and sizes range between, and often international organizations offer local chapters that function similarly to smaller peer groups.

By meeting regularly and sharing problems, concerns, and successes, owners of growing businesses provide insight, guidance, and support to one another. No two members need be in the same business. While a group within your business has obvious advantages, a more diverse group may be less apt to get bogged down in the nitty-gritty of the trade and instead can delve into the details of infrastructure, personnel, marketing, financial, and customer issues.

If you prefer a group of business owners within your industry, trade groups exist for almost any business you can think of. If there isn't one for you, consider starting one. Some industries in which an entrepreneur may feel isolated in creating or growing the operation, such as freelancing and virtual or home-based businesses, have access to groups that share resources and offer tremendous support. Other groups that meet to support and advise center around a common vision or set of values such as eco-friendly or natural product businesses. Many businesses are supporting common causes and sharing in similar struggles. These organizations are stronger together than alone and have an interest in helping each other thrive.

One successful international organization, built on the peer advisory board concept, is the Women Presidents' Organization (WPO), established as a resource for women who own businesses grossing over one million dollars for services and three million for products. The message is that a business owner is never beyond learning from his/her peers. This group, with chapters through the U.S. and internationally, offers successful women business owners the opportunity to problem-solve with others who have built thriving businesses. Chapters function as peer advisory boards as well as resources. The concept expands beyond the small group with national and international conferences and business building events.

For formal or informal in-person or online meetings, establish a meeting format, ground rules, and a time frame. Whether your peer advisory group is face-to-face or virtual, a few standard ground rules apply.

Ground rules for peer advisory groups:

- **Be honest.** If you "put on a happy face" and make your finances, employees, or other issues seem brighter than they are, you won't get the help that you need.
- **Listen.** Don't go in with an "I've tried it all before" attitude. You will not only miss out on receiving valuable input; you will give other members the message that you don't want it, and they may pull back from sharing.
- **Be direct, yet gentle.** Yes, Suzanne can't keep a powerful sales force and, although she doesn't know why, it's very clear to the rest of you. Be diplomatic, ask questions, lead her to the realization.
- **Remain supportive.** Don't just throw out a solution and move on to the next problem. Leave time to follow through.

Meeting topics may include one or a mix of the following:

- Discuss current business issues that affect all members.
- Discuss business strategies that are useful to all members.
- Draw upon specific members' skills and knowledge for presentations to the group.
- Ask individual members to present case studies of problems they face for the group to solve.
- Ask individual members to present success stories from which the group can learn.
- Read and discuss current business literature.

Figure 11.2: FORMATS FOR PEER ADVISORY BOARD MEETINGS

Generally, the most successful approach to advisory board meetings is mixing and matching formats over a period of time.

1. Each meeting focuses on one member's issue(s). The next meeting begins with a brief "How is it going?" follow-up and then focuses on the next person.

2. Within a two-hour meeting for four people, each one gets to present an issue for a half-hour discussion (five-minute framing, twenty-five-minute discussion).

3. The group conducts site visits so all members can see the others' work environments and meet staff. Visits during working hours are ideal; however, even after-work visits help set the scene.

These meeting formats were developed by peer advisory boards launched by Grow Smart, a business-building program created for the New Jersey Association of Women Business Owners (NJAWBO).

QUICK Tip

Tailor your group to your needs: One winter morning a few years ago, Lisa Bell realized she could use some critical insights to grow Global Connections Speakers Bureau, a home-based business in Coconut Creek, Florida. She found the work-at-home environment isolating, and attending meetings at the chamber of commerce, National Association of Women Business Owners, or Meeting Planners International did not fulfill Bell's need for business critiquing.

So Bell and four small business compatriots sat near a pond, opened a bottle of champagne, and let the ideas, news, successes, and concerns flow. What they created was a MasterMind group, so named by Napoleon Hill, author of the classic business book, *Think and Grow Rich.*

The participants now dedicate about four hours to uninterrupted meeting, giving each member time to float ideas, concerns, successes, or any item in need of feedback. The group uses the meetings to foster inspiration, instruction, and motivation, or just "recharge our batteries"—all in a comfortable, confidential setting, Bell said.

—From "Mastermind Groups Help Build Self & Business" by Jeff Zbar, chiefhomeofficer.com

Create an Outside Expert Advisory Board

Outside advice is extremely valuable. You get a fresh perspective from one or more people who are not immersed in the day-to-day activities of your business. A number of growing businesses create advisory boards by tapping into the talent that they see around them. Several options exist for those growing their businesses.

As you network and get to know executives and business owners you admire, think about whom you would want on an advisory board for your company. First, carefully frame the responsibilities and limits of your advisory board members. You want to solicit advice, not relinquish control. Also, you are pulling in busy people, so have a tight agenda with substantial issues.

Remember that your advisory board, no matter what the size or composition, is another team on which you participate. All the rules apply. Ensure that this team works smoothly together for a common goal: helping your business grow and succeed.

QUICK Tip

Stack the deck: An advisory board for a small company serves double duty. Of course, we looked to them for personal financial investment and the ability to introduce us to contacts that would be interested in funding our business plan. However, what was much more important to us was the board candidate's ability to offer time and advice based on experience.

CPR (Creative Products Resource) needed advisors that had worked in the consumer products industry and understood the needs of a company launching a project into the market. We needed advisors with corporate knowledge, financial strategy acumen, and the capacity to act as sounding boards in the variety of areas that we would be entering.

The candidates we invited to join us were professionals with solid corporate experience but who also expressed enthusiasm for the entrepreneurial experience. All of our board members agreed to be available by phone whenever we needed them in between board meetings and to attend the quarterly meetings for the full time necessary.

We selected a person who had been a director of new products for a major company because of his excitement over innovation. We selected a person who had been president of his own company that had gone public because he understood the challenges of the complicated journey from private to public. We selected an investment banker who had counseled many companies through their ventures and understood the impact of a business plan's financial strategies. We also chose a board member specifically because he did not come from the industry but had extensive business and managerial skills; he could offer a perspective different from his codirectors.

Our goal was to put together a group that would advise us carefully, respect and build on each other's input, and concentrate on our business issues at each stage of our company's evolution.

—Betty Jagoda Murphy, cofounder ReGenesis LLC

Client/Customer Advisory Boards

Anyone who is potentially in the market for your product or service qualifies as an advisory board member. Wondering what customers want? Ask them. The Internet provides more opportunity than ever to create customer feedback forums, discussion groups, and chat rooms to test run ideas and solicit comments. You might choose to make your customer advisory board "official" by having members sign up. Consider creating a blog that offers customers a steady flow of information and creates ongoing interest. This could be a good source for finding customer advisors, holding their interest, and inviting input. Keep blog entries steady. Set a schedule you can keep. Entries can be brief, but keep that blog alive. If it doesn't change for three weeks, readers may lose interest.

You may choose to create a smaller, screened customer advisory board and offer small perks or advanced notices in exchange for feedback and practical ideas, but in this virtual world of ours, customers are "checking in" with interesting sites day and night. Catch their attention.

QUICK Tip

Bring in your audience: Most kids walk into Build-A-Bear to create their own customized stuffed animals. Many come home with a little something more: Maxine Clark's business card. Clark, the company's founder and CEO, visits two to three of her two-hundred-plus stores a week, helping customers, chatting with employees, and, yeah, networking with preteens. "I'm on a lot of online buddy lists," she says.

Besides a pair of sore thumbs, what does Clark get out of all this customer correspondence? "Ideas," she says. "I used to feel like I had to come up with all the ideas myself, but it's so much easier relying on my customers." The list of customer suggestions that have made their way onto shelves is always growing—from bear accessories like mini-scooters to mascot bears sold at sports stadiums.

To tap into customer reactions to those new ideas, Clark asks for feedback from her "virtual cub advisory council," a community of children on her email list. Scouting out a new location, Clark will email council members in an area to ask them which malls they shop at most. She'll poll her network to see if the latest trend she's spotted in New York—say, metallic sequined purses—might be worth rolling out as bear accoutrements.

—Excerpt from: "Customer-Centered Leader: Maxine Clark," by Lucas Conley, October, 2005, *Fast Company* magazine, fastcompany.com

Growth Strategies

As the owner of a growing business, you watch your cash flow carefully. You know you need help, but adding full- or even part-time staff is not a viable choice at the moment. Is it hire or go it alone? Not by a long shot. Many successful businesses have grown by augmenting human resources through avenues that won't deplete financial resources.

Subcontracting

Subcontracting can play a significant role in a growing business. Service businesses often use subcontractors on a per project basis. Keeping a full-time staff of computer technicians, technical writers, or training professionals could "break the bank"; however, having a team of professionals who can work with you on special projects at a moment's notice enables you to serve your clients and manage your resources. Companies that work successfully with subcontractors create a team environment from the outset. Subcontractors must project your company's mission and values and are your embodiment to everyone they work with. This means clear expectations and ongoing communication. Feedback from your field team is essential for successful growth.

The best way to ensure a smooth working relationship is to have a clear contract with terms to which you and your subcontractors agree. Share your mission, vision, and values. Discuss your goals for the project(s) they will work on and get their input. The more integral a part of your team the subcontractor is, the more comfortable your client will be. You want clear project guidelines and a mechanism for discussing changes that the client may request of your subcontractor.

Clarify appropriate and inappropriate roles and responsibilities. You may put a technical writer into a pharmaceutical company to work on standard operating procedures and learn that she's in the midst of an internal "political" battle. She may be working side-by-side with a disgruntled employee who dislikes the project leader or an employee who is outspoken about his problems with the project's direction and looking for allies. No matter how closely she works with her on-site team, she must steer clear of taking sides or voicing opinions in that environment. Often, the business owner cannot anticipate the problems that might arise. Do your best to clarify your expectations. Ask behavioral questions about previous assignments. Stress to subcontractors that they are representing your company.

Stay Involved

As with any team member, you cannot release a subcontractor into a client relationship and then move on. You don't want to micromanage, but you do want to receive regular reports of how the work is progressing and any other client feedback or subcontractor feedback that will help you support this subcontractor. If face-to-face meetings are impossible, ensure steady email contact and periodic telephone conversations.

Some subcontractors work side-by-side with employees. This occurs frequently in technical companies or with technical personnel in nontechnical companies. Others may be the "outside team," occasionally working at your site. They might be a sales force, a training team, or other service provider. These are not second-class citizens. They are your bread and butter. Often, office staff may view them as prima donnas or "high maintenance." Your responsibility as a business owner is to ensure that everyone who represents your company is part of you team and treated as such. Subcontractors are valuable company assets and need to know that they are supported.

Ensure that your subcontractors are bona fide subcontractors. Know and communicate clear, legal guidelines that define these relationships. Check with your attorney and your accountant to ensure you are covering all bases.

Joint Ventures/Strategic Alliances

You may be growing more rapidly than your current human resources can manage. One option is forming a joint venture or strategic alliance with a colleague for a particular line of business or for projects with one or several clients.

Select a joint venture or strategic alliance partner who:
- Complements your strengths
- Shares your values and ethics
- Has a similar approach to client relations and problem solving
- Has the same priorities regarding cost/benefit analysis, staffing, and quality

Often, an opportunity is "suddenly there" and you don't have time for a long courtship. Reaching out to someone you know, someone with whom you've worked, or at the very least, someone who comes highly recommended by a source you trust increases the chances for success.

No matter how well you know and trust your potential short-term partner, put your agreement in writing. The more valuable the friendship/relationship is to you, the more important the written agreement becomes. It can save the friendship.

QUICK Tip

Collaborate: I periodically collaborate with another consulting firm as a way of developing my own. The group is comprised of other consultants and business owners with very diverse backgrounds. We work together a few times a year with specific clients and are able to immediately function as a very effective team. It is a selfless experience in which egos are never an issue and each of us can rely on any other to lend support, solutions, and the latest industry knowledge. Simply put, this continues to be the best team that I have ever worked with, regardless of the member configuration or work content. I always look forward to working with this team, and it always exceeds my expectations. We all engage in complete collaboration from start to finish.

—Georgann Occhipinti, president, Diamond Associates, Milford, NJ, www.diamondtraining.com

Mergers/Acquisitions

Many small companies find that combining with another company is a way to grow. Common paths are the merger and the acquisition. The process for either one is lengthy and requires you to work closely with an attorney and an accountant. Good business dictates that you keep your financial house in order and your records accurate. The due diligence necessary for this level of business transaction is detailed and carefully delineated. Because you never know when the opportunity or the need may present itself, maintain records as though such a transaction is imminent. That way, your preparation when the time comes will not be overwhelming.

The merger is the union between two business entities. You might decide that you and a colleague or a competitor might do best to join forces rather than till the same field separately. Mergers are complex arrangements with a myriad of choices for implementation. They bring equity of equal or unequal value; either way, a business structure should be adopted or created that best suits both companies.

The acquisition is as clear as it sounds, one company acquiring another. You may find that as you grow, you and your team would fare better financially by flying under someone else's flag. The flip side is that you may realize that acquiring companies smaller than yours will fuel your company's growth. Occasionally, small companies exploring the possibility of being acquired realize that their best interest is served by acquiring.

External Resources

Your external team provides knowledge and resources that often lie outside the realm of the typical business owner. Even if you are great with numbers, a professional accountant keeps up with changes that might positively or adversely affect your business. We don't advocate an extensive, expensive entourage; however, key professionals will save you money and problems. The key to having a strong external team is maintaining those relationships when you are not in crisis mode. You want them to know who you are and to care about your success.

A Strong Banking Relationship

A strong banking relationship can keep your business going. Do you ever wonder how a business mogul like Donald Trump can go into debt one week and announce his business expansion based on a multimillion-dollar loan the next? He has spent decades fostering trusting banking relationships.

On a smaller scale, every business owner needs a trusted banker. Those who advise business start-ups always suggest immediately borrowing a small amount of money that you don't need and don't intend to use. Then, pay it back on time. Repeat this scenario with a larger amount. You have begun to establish a banking relationship. Get to know specific people: the bank manager, the loan officer, the platform personnel. Every bank is different; however, most respect their good clients and want to help them succeed. Some banks are more in tune with growing companies' needs. Network with others in business and compare banking services and relationships.

You know that large contract will come in if you can afford the extra people power to pull it off. Share your contract with your banker, explain your time frame, structure an appropriate line of credit to ensure that you can always meet payroll. As long as you hold up your end of the bargain, your banker will be there to help you out. Many of us have had those times when expenses outpaced income, and we needed a little help to get through the lean times. If you always paid back your small loans and stayed up-to-date with your line of credit, asking for a higher ceiling is not like asking for the moon.

An Accountant

Your accountant is, in a sense, your navigator. Many business owners think that they don't have the time or the money to meet periodically with an accountant. If you are among them, think again. The accountant who is on top of your business issues can guide you through expense decisions, tax issues, even hiring verses subcontracting decisions. A good accountant knows what questions to ask and doesn't rely upon the client to expect the financial riptides and shoals that could ensnare them. For example, you may be working with a client in another state. You may not realize that you have to pay taxes in that state as well. Your accountant should know to ask where your clients are located. Following are just a few of the things that you should consider discussing with your accountant. The more informed and proactive you are, the more effective your result will be. Do the little things that help you avoid big problems later.

Here are some questions that, according to your specific business needs, you should discuss with your accountant.

- What are the tax implications of working in specific other states?
- What are the tax implications of online sales?
- Are you familiar with state and federal guidelines for using independent contractors?
  - Are there special conditions if any of them work on W4s for other employers?
  - Should they be treated as employees or subcontractors?
  - Should they be provided liability insurance coverage, or should they have their own?
  - Do subcontractors need to bill on letterhead?
- What is needed for international work?

Consider other things you may be doing that an accountant should know about. Ask your accountant, "What else should I be considering?"

An Attorney

Your attorney's job isn't to get you out of trouble. It's to keep you out of trouble. Your attorney can do this if you keep him/her apprised of your goals and plans. Attorneys know of laws, roadblocks, and how to find the clear passages. Your knowledge of these can prevent missteps, financial losses, and lawsuits. Prevention is always less costly than the cure. Work with your attorney to draft fair (win-win) contracts for employment, subcontracting, and leases.

An attorney's knowledge of the law as it relates to employment, immigration, discrimination, disability, liability, insurance, copyrights and patents, the Occupational Safety and Health Administration (OSHA), and safety allows you to focus on the business of your business with a clear mind. Seek advice before embarking on a new course: an expansion, a merger, an acquisition, property leasing or purchase, or letting an employee go. By consulting with your attorney on a number of these areas, you can have processes and paperwork in place to facilitate going forward without needing to worry about negative legal repercussions.

Even if someone hands you something and says it's "standard," let your attorney be the judge. Never begin a conversation with your attorney with: "I just signed…"

Professional Teambuilders

Much teambuilding can be done, as you've seen, on your own and within a small business budget. If you want to continue to run your own teambuilding exercises, you can find a number of supplementary exercises on the Internet. However, professional teambuilding companies can offer a myriad of programs and consulting services that can only serve to strengthen the bonds and sense of team you've created.

Beyond what you can do in-house, many creative teambuilding companies and independent consultants offer highly effective programs. You might have a teambuilding program tailored to your team and your immediate needs or a consultant working in a hands-on way to energize your team and help the team take shape and set a course for action. Other teambuilding professionals will moderate teambuilding exercises, possibly taking your team out to build a team bond in unconventional ways. These out-of-the-box approaches are best implemented by professionals who will help your team translate what was learned to the practicalities of their daily routines and interactions. Going into these programs as a team-conscious business owner will ensure that your team will get the most from any teambuilding intervention. You can help with the follow-up and transfer of lessons learned to the practical work setting.

Still, you want to be careful in assessing a potential teambuilding company. Find out how long the company has been in business. Do they have a track record with customizing teambuilding sessions, consultations, and events to fit customer needs? Ask for references.

What sense do you get from discussing your needs with this company's owner or representative? Does the company understand your needs? Does the facilitator? Do they have solid backgrounds that show you they understand how teambuilding relates, in a practical way, to the daily activities of your business? Will they customize their activities to your industry and company? Sure, they can help your team leap through the jungle, but can they help people apply the experience, or is the mental leap going to seem like a stretch to your team? These programs run the risk of seeming cheesy or ludicrous if their practical application is not apparent.

Does the company have comprehensive public liability insurance? If the company is taking groups out on teambuilding excursions, insurance is a standard item. Consider, also, that the fact that an insurance company's approval adds to credibility.

Do they have an array of options available? If a company runs one specialized event, your possibilities narrow; find a company that offers teambuilding activities or retreats and runs conferences and incentive-based events. The more options available, the more a company can help you tailor a teambuilding program to your needs.

It's all about teams: "In my role as an internal consultant, almost every request I have received to assist both intact and extended work groups (teams) has been for assistance in solving a work-related (technical process) problem. Yet in every instance, my research in preparation for those interventions uncovered the problem not to be of a technical nature, but in the group's ability to work together toward that end. Specifically, they consistently identified their problems as being in the area of team leadership, communication, and trust. (In fact, they identified their technical expertise as a strength.) Although improving the group's ability to function in these 'softer' competencies is a difficult task, developing and implementing action plans that address team issues consistently achieves measurable results."

—Peter Tomolonis is a consultant based in Metuchen, NJ, www.petertomolonis.com

Remember the Home Team

Entrepreneurs must be careful not to shortchange their businesses, their teams, and their clients—so when something must fall through the cracks, it's personal. Sports teams talk about the "home team advantage," but in business the home team is often at a disadvantage. During the various stages of growth, many business owners and managers may begin to take it for granted.

As you take your team to the next level, remember that your most important stakeholders are those who are part of your life dreams. Family and friends who are your support system and your personal cheering section deserve your appreciation for the part they play in facilitating your professional endeavors. They are critical to your well-being and the energy that makes you the successful person you are. You turn to them as sounding boards, advisors, and fill-ins for the pieces of your life that you may have to periodically give short shrift—cooking, errands, being there for everything and everyone you wish you could. They pitch in with favors large and small, as small as reminding you to breathe. These are the "stakeholders" who know who you are, not just what you do, and their stake is not only in your success but in your happiness and well-being.

If your busy schedule keeps you from feeling human or connecting with the people who matter most in your world, put some energy into finding small ways to reach out and possibly restructuring to allow some of that work/life balance you allow your team. You are an entrepreneur, not a machine. Make time for those who provide a space where you can be yourself, free to laugh, cry, and love. Schedule a time to call that friend, the one you never have time for but both of your spirits are uplifted when you connect. Those closest to you need to know that you appreciate their efforts and support, and they need to know they can expect the same of you—a helping hand, a sounding board, a soft place to land.

Appendix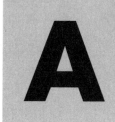

Reflect and Compare

If you have not used all of the team activities, we encourage you to go back to them as you continue the team-building process. We recommend that you complete the following team assessment to gauge how far you've come through working with this book. Of course, putting activities and ideas into practice is the key to change, and, if you are still in the process of doing so, you may want to take this assessment now and then again in a few months. After you've completed it, compare your score and Team Profile with the baseline you established with the assessment you completed at the outset. Has there been significant improvement?

Leadership Activity: Assess Your Team

Answer each of the following with a score of 1, 2, or 3.

1 = True   2 = Sometimes True   3 = Not True for Our Team

Organization

1. The team knows exactly what has to get done.
2. Each member of the team has a clear idea of the team goals.
3. Team members are clear about their roles within the team.
4. The team holds regular, effective meetings.

Supportive Atmosphere

5. Team members who offer new ideas get a lot of support and encouragement.
6. Team members freely express their real views.
7. All team members demonstrate respect for each other.
8. Everyone's opinion gets listened to.
9. There is healthy debate among team members but very little bickering.

Methods for Troubleshooting and Change

10. The team has clear channels for concerns or complaints.
11. The team has a working method for resolving conflict.
12. If a team member leaves or is suddenly out sick, other team members know how to access key information and can pick up critical pieces.
13. Team members are open to new ideas.
14. Team members don't arbitrarily discard what is working for something just because it's new.

Team Spirit

15. Team members are excited about the project/mission/goals.
16. Team member know that they each play a valuable part in the project/mission/goals.
17. Team members understand that challenges are opportunities to make improvements, be creative, and use their talents and abilities to the fullest.

What's the Score?

17–24 Congratulations! You are an outstanding leader with a strong team. Celebrate with your team, and acknowledge their success!

25–35 Congratulations! You've earned a good score. Continue to work with the exercises, and, when your score improves, celebrate with your team!

If you scored higher than a 35, don't despair, especially if your score has shown some improvement. Change takes time. Continue to work with the exercises and implement the proven guidelines in the book. Check the assessment for areas where you had the most 3s, then the most 2s. Revisit those areas in this book and explore further resources for strengthening your team in those areas.

Fill in your new team profile.

Team Profile

Team Strengths:

_____
_____
_____
_____

What can I do to build and capitalize on these strengths?

_____
_____
_____

Team Challenges:

_____
_____
_____
_____

What can I do to help my team and individual team members overcome these challenges?

_____
_____
_____

Looking Ahead

How has your profile changed from the beginning? Don't be concerned if you still have the same *number* of team challenges; if you have *different* challenges, that shows progress. As you climb to each new level, each has its challenges.

Take some time, if you haven't already, to follow up on outcomes from your team and leadership exercises. As you go forward, you may want to continue to integrate some of the activities in this book into your team-building process, so we included an "Activity Reference" chart in Appendix B for easy reference.

We wish you success as you continue to streamline your team for greater and greater results.

Appendix

Activity Reference

Throughout this book, we've emphasized that strong teams result from effective leadership, open communication, and well-earned trust. That's the framework. You can hone team skills, increase energy, and enhance teamwork by introducing teambuilding exercises. Just as exercise strengthens our muscles and our minds, engaging your team in focused activities will broaden individual perspectives and strengthen the group.

We created the following Activity Reference to simplify finding the teambuilding activities that are right for you and your team.

CHAPTER	ACTIVITY	LEADERSHIP	TEAM
1	Letting Go	*	
	Assess Your Team	*	
2	Why Are We Here		*
	Are You a Collaborator?		*
	Amoeba Race		*
	How Are We Doing?		*
	What Stage Is Your Team In?	*	
3	Brainstorming		*
	The Wooden Dowel		*
	Devil's Advocate		*
	Action Planning		*
	Assuming Assumptions Can Be Useful		*
	Alternative Scenarios		*
	The Ad Hoc Book Club		*
	Create Your Own		*
4	Listening Self-Test	*	
	Listening		*
	Self-Assessment: Perceptions/ Comfort Zones		*
	Group Mandala		*
	Meeting Mania		*
5	Following the Seven-Step Feedback Model	*	
	Building Egos for Team Strength		*
	Learning Curve		*
	Watch Your Language	*	
	Sports		*

6	What Are Your Expectations?		*
	What Do You Know about Yourself and Others on Your Team?		*
	Create Your Own Culture		*
7	Risk/Benefit Analysis	*	
	The World Around You	*	
	Change Visions		*
	Ties	*	
	The Change Connection		*
	Change Is		*
8	Communication Profile		*
9	SWOT Analysis	*	
	How Are We Doing?		*
	Know Your Team	*	
	Product and Service Assessment		*
	Stakeholder Identification and Analysis	*	
10	KSAs	*	
	Leadership Activity	*	
	Legal Question Quiz	*	
	Creating the Best Fit		*

Index

About the Authors

Linda Eve Diamond designed, wrote, and conducted training programs for Diamond Associates and is now a full-time freelance writer and author of several business books.

Harriet Diamond, freelance writer and author of seven business books, founded Diamond Associates, a training and consulting company that delivers teambuilding, change, and customer service solutions. She serves on the advisory board of *Enterprising Women*, a magazine for women business owners.